DEMYSTIFYING MAGIC NEW WITCH FUNDAMENTALS

*Starter guide to paganism, finding your craft
and the true power of spellcasting*

KENNEDY BLACK

Contents

Introduction

What makes you feel drawn to magic?

Do you look to the horizon, the full moon, or the wildlife around, and feel something twitch deep inside? Does something linger just below the surface of it all and make you want to dive in and explore beyond the surface?

Do you simply feel that there must be more than what you see around you?

You're not alone. We can all sense there is a deeper knowing underneath it all, that much more exists within our reality, we can feel it gently pulling at us. Magic appeals to a broad range of people who feel the same way. They want a more meaningful, committed and disciplined life pulled to discover something more profound and wonderful than the everyday. Like you, they could feel a hidden world and choose to zero in on that something deeper waiting inside their heart and begin a magical journey.

Magic works like a long hike up a steep yet gorgeous mountain. You have many options for your path and all of them lead up to the summit. Which path you take – your pace up the mountainside and what you stop to see, smell and eat – all depend on you. Unlike many other religions, there are only broad guides to magic, not step-by-step instructions. You have to use your intellect, your creativity, and intuition to find shelter, build strength, and learn from each step as you climb higher and higher.

That "more" so many people feel is a new level of spirituality, something that allows for invention and their own personal signature. Creating and casting spells, building rituals, meditating, and communing with nature help us find our own niche in magic and connect with ourselves and the deep, beautiful well of power that we all carry. The incredible thing about magic is that it lives in every person and it's constantly available for the taking.

All you have to do is look inside and find it.

A lot of people start with a problem they want to solve. They want to develop their own resilience, learn to accept themselves, stop feeling weak in the face of their adversaries, or live free from the latest family drama. Like them, you're ready to commit to the development of your own personal power, but where do you start?

This book is here for you as a good primer. If you don't understand any of the symbolism, terminology, or even the intentions behind magic, this is the book for you. Rather than focusing on how to make your new, flowy robe or cast a dangerous, unpredictable spell, this book looks at the all important fundamentals.

This book can prepare for sweeping changes in your life. The things you want to achieve are within reach with the help of magical practice, but it takes commitment, knowledge, and integrity to master. This book can get you through that difficult journey. It can inspire you on every level and change your basic frequency, (i.e. how you feel on a spiritual level), so you can shift your vibrations and benefit others around you.

This text draws from a wealth of knowledge and experience thanks to centuries of practicing mystics who recorded their discoveries for future students. While your journey won't directly reflect anyone else's perfectly, each previous teacher can inform and guide you along your own path up that magical mountain. Each one will also help you stay safe and learn how to build up patience with yourself and, by association, the divine powers around you. Reaching that profound, powerful place inside yourself and building up your own divinity is something that comes with endless rewards. It's worth the effort.

You might feel tempted to jump to the end; to attempt a big, powerful spell well beyond your abilities, or that puts you in danger. This temptation is understandable. Magic is exciting! The thought of doing something transformative can make us consider ditching the climb altogether and just act as if we're at our goal instead of truly earning it. This act cheats nobody but you. When you try to take shortcuts, you can only reap short-term superficial rewards that can lead to something dangerous. This book will help you stay protected and make better choices while harnessing this incredible, beautiful power.

And its beauty is endless. Magic exists in every moment of our lives, each is an opportunity to learn something, to reflect on changes in our lives, to take the opportunity to understand something deeper about ourselves. Used properly, it can make your life exponentially better. We'll also explore how magic is embedded within scientific principles. You may have already read about the Universal Laws, similar to what you may have studied in physics class. However, we will explore the magical take on these laws and uncover the hidden meaning that governs your life. For example, the Law of Cause and Effect simply states that every action has a reaction. The Law of Attraction states that wherever we put our attention - on our career, on our spiritual growth, our family - is where we'll start to see rewards.

Like physics class, magical practice puts a huge emphasis on balance. While magical practice does this less tangibly or measurably, the principles are the same. If we take something from the earth, we have to give something back. If we want more love in our lives, we have to give love first.

Anyone who wants to lead a more magical lifestyle needs to go through a transition first. You must accept that this won't be easy but with commitment, integrity, and the right intention you may find yourself living a much more meaningful life. This book will help you make that shift and show you some of the different paths you can choose to continue on your way. It will let you know where you need to do some additional research or practice and what it means when something doesn't resonate with you and how to recognize your true spiritual expression.

Remember, magic will always challenge you and ask you to keep reflecting and growing. This book will help you take those first steps and move away from a life that no longer inspires you.

You have to set your mind to change and to operate from a higher level of consciousness to grow and transform into something new. That is the spirit of magic, as this book will prove.

Don't forget, this book is not meant to force you to one craft over another but rather to help form your practice without the pressures of any doctrine or set of rules. Follow what speaks to you and seek out the right path for you and your craft. Use each of these to find what is important to you and use them to develop your own unique power.

Let this book act as your protective doorway into a new, deeper way of living and your guide to an incredible, new reality. All you have to do is say yes and step through.

Now, let's begin.

CHAPTER 1

What Is Magic?

Many individuals who believe in magic believe that there is a type of exaggerated showmanship that comes along with the practice. Magic is much more humble. It is a practice that is much more personal and used to advance the lives of individuals rather than entertain for commercialism. While you can play and have fun with magic, the real kind of magic is found within reality. It is a power that is developed internally through connections between the self and the physical world. We are all born with the ability and power to use magic but our realization of this power has been pulled from us due to culture and education. Instead, we are told that religions are the only mystical systems available to us and are taught to obey a hierarchy of power that is beyond ourselves; whether that hierarchy is mystically based or not. We have been distracted and made to believe that magic, derived deep within ourselves, does not exist. To truly understand what magic means, what it looks like, and how it is used in our reality, we must take a step back and explore the spiritual movement of paganism and the newly popularized neo-paganism. It is through these three spiritual movements that magic truly thrives.

History of Paganism

To first understand paganism, we should look at the ancient definition and conception of the religion as well as where the word comes from. First, the words 'Pagan' and 'Paganism' have been derived from the Latin word pagus. Pagus and its other variations refer to the ancient Roman administrative term designating a rural subdivision of tribal territory. The modern equivalent is the word "hick."

Ironically, the hicks of the world were originally seen as the educated, informed groups of the world. They followed a polytheistic system - a belief that each part of life is ruled by a different god. The god of the forest, the god of rain, the sun god, each part of nature and social life had a god and these gods demanded sacrifices. People saw their deities as intrinsic to a good, fulfilling life and happily made regular sacrifices to keep those gods satisfied.

The original Christians started as a small group in the first century during the Roman Empire, and they were vastly outnumbered. They wanted to change how people believed and preached the idea of one god and salvation which were two completely new concepts. Their approach to religion with a sacrifice-free life and a beautiful afterlife caught on and by the end of the 4th century, Christians numbered over 30 million people.[1]

As Christianity grew in popularity, followers insisted that anyone who worshipped multiple gods practiced an evil or even satanic

[1] https://www.history.com/news/inside-the-conversion-tactics-of-the-early-christian-church

religion. Pagans were pushed further and further to the margins of society where they could easily be maligned and blamed for any particular problem. Those not willing to convert to the new church evolved into what we now think of as pagans.

But what does paganism practice?

What Is Paganism?

Paganism is a deeply traditional and ancient practice that encourages individuals to seek out and pursue the divine based on their own experience rather than through a predetermined doctrine or scripture. Three characteristics make a religion pagan: nature-based, multiple deities, and the idea of the female God.

Nature-Based

First, paganism focuses on the veneration and reverence to the natural world around individuals rather than only focusing on otherworldly deities. This great respect and worship towards that natural world are marked by practices, rituals, and festivals that allow individuals to give thanks and ask for favor and virtue.

One example of how pagans use the natural world as the basis of worship is the four seasons of the year. Pagans consider the cycle of moving through the summer, fall, winter, and spring to be representative of the changes, challenges, growth, and death cycles that humans go through in their lives. Pagans celebrate certain rituals and festivals to mark each of the seasons and bring good fortune to both themselves and the whole of humanity.

Multiple Deities

Paganism allows for the worshiping of multiple deities. What makes these deities even more special is that they are gods representative and closely linked to aspects of nature. Taking a note from the gods of ancient times and before the development of the Judeo-Christian religion, pagan gods were each associated with an aspect of nature or of the natural world.

Female Gods

For Christianity and Judaism, the face and personification of God is male. However, for paganism, the personification is usually female because of the close relationship between the gods and nature. Such an idea is seen in the term Mother Nature who gives birth to all living things on earth.

Other Aspects of Paganism

Of course, there are other characteristics of paganism that should be mentioned.

Pagans believe that the divine gifts are expressed and found in our everyday lives, rather than imposed on us from the beyond. For example, pagans will examine everyday events to receive signs from the divine and communicate with the spiritual forces from other realms. These patterns can be found in the migration of animals, reading tea leaves, or looking at rock formations to receive messages from the divine.

There is also a sense of self-responsibility when it comes to paganism. Followers are encouraged to take full responsibility for their actions. Further on in the book, we will explore natural laws which are the laws of the universe that govern our world and nurtures your inner being. Many pagans and mystics know that those universal and natural laws emphasize that our actions have consequences that flow in a continuous series. This makes pagans environmentalists as well as they work to preserve and respect the land. Many of the rituals and spells used within paganism show reverence and appreciation to the natural world from which we harvest and rely on for survival.

Generally speaking, pagans follow the belief that there is a world beyond our own that can influence our actions and can aid us in times of need when called upon. Pagans believe the communication between our world and the worlds beyond – the world of the divine – is one of constant communication and all one person must do is practice how to look for such signs of communication in our world.

What Is Neo-Paganism?

Neo-paganism is a modern-day interpretation of the classical practices of paganism. It is difficult to make generalizations about such a practice as there is no central and universal authority. Instead, each neo-pagan – or group – practices slightly differently. That being said, if we trace the origins of this religious and mystical practice we can get a clearer picture of what this practice entails.

Neo-paganism came about in the 1960s. Some scholars attribute this movement in response to the counter-culture and political situation at the time which encouraged a return to nature. Similar to the historical religion of paganism, neo-paganism has some identifying features due to the time that it was created. However, there are key differences between traditional paganism and neo- paganism. While they both were developed as a sort of rebellion against politics and religion, neo-paganism developed some of the philosophies of its traditional counterpart into a new religion. The following are some aspects and philosophies that neo-paganism developed over time:

To Affirm Life

To begin, the neo-pagan is a life-affirming practitioner. This means that they treat life as an adventure in itself rather than looking to and preparing for their death. This way of thinking, which treats life as an adventure, differs from many other religions that dictate how you are meant to live your life. Pagans choose to live in the present and focus on daily life, without any worry about their afterlife.

Return To Nature

There is (again) A Return To Nature in neo-paganism. Neopagans consider themselves to be interconnected with nature and that nature itself is connected to all living things in their world. As a result, they consider nature to be sacred and a source from which all magic is derived. Based on this belief, many neopagans wish to preserve nature and the environment in general to respect and nurture its power.

Re-Enhancement and Re-Enchantment

Neopagans feel that humans have become disconnected from the world. Many humans, through the lens of neo-paganism, give in to the superficial distractions of our society. For example, many individuals simply go through the motions of life, being obsessed with work and focused on material gain, not enjoying every moment, and are unaware of how powerful they are. As a result, neo-pagans wish to bring a sort of re-enhancement to humans and reconnect with the world around them.

Pantheism

Similar to traditional paganism, neo-paganism also follows multiple gods and goddesses. Rather than pray and devote themselves to one deity, neopagans experience multiple gods and beings of higher and deeper power, based on different elements of nature.

Goddess and Divine Feminine

Neo-pagans believe divinity is something that transcends gender. While other religions focus on a single male deity, neopagans see their beings of divinity often represented as feminine or lacking gender entirely.

Intentional Ritual

While neo-pagans give up the traditional form of praying, they do hold steadfast to intention and ritual. Rather than praying every night or in times of need to a single deity, they scheduled rituals performed at specific times of the year to bring about certain results and events in their lives. For example, neo-pagans celebrate and have rituals that fall on the equinoxes and the solstices every year. These rituals are created by each practicing pagan and are specific to the intention and goal of the individual. While traditional pagans also celebrate equinoxes and solstices, the neo- pagan celebrations are far less strict and rigid in their praying and rituals that take place during these celebrations. The intentions differ as well. With the development of different technologies in our world, the neo-pagan celebrations involve a sort of return to nature, turning away from technology that the traditional celebrations did not.

Darkness

As mentioned above, paganism is a religion that focuses on life and does not necessarily prepare the individual for their afterlife. However, this does not mean that neo-pagans avoid and fear death. Instead, they embrace the concept. Neo-pagans believe that there is power in the darkness of life and a sense of calm that comes with understanding and accepting the darkness and the inevitable death of humans. Just as nature has a beautiful and dark side, so does life. Rather than fear this darkness, the neo-pagans embrace it.

Pluralism in Beliefs

One of the last beliefs that neo-pagans hold is the idea of pluralism in the world. The neo-pagan sees and understands the diversity and non-singular characteristics of life and nature. They do not hold onto any universal truths or belief systems that discriminate against otherness. For example, sexism and racism are both beliefs that hold truths about one type of person and discredit others. For neo-pagans, sexism and racism are abhorrent and neo-pagans believe in allowing for differences in beliefs and individuals.

Like paganism, neo-paganism is a religion that differentiates itself from any other monotheistic religion. It came out of a time of revolution and 1960s counter-culture and brings the individual back to focusing on nature and the world we live in. Relying on and performing rituals, the neo-pagan draws their power from their relationship with nature.

What Is Magic?

So what is magic?

The task of defining such a concept is a difficult task because there are technically two different conceptions of magic. The first is a fictional type of magic found in storybooks and movies, while the latter is a more subtle and tangible type of magic that exists within our world. These two definitions of the same word create contention and confusion. The popularity of the former type of magic was so pervasive that Wiccans chose to write and refer to their magic with a 'k' at the end to differentiate themselves.[2] What makes the differentiation between these two concepts difficult is that they stem from the same base definition. Both terms mean that which is hidden or not yet understood. Magic is the power to influence energy or bring about certain events by the manipulation or change in human perspective. The movement or direction universal energy will alter the projection of reality.

---

[2] "A Wiccan Guide to Magic: What Is Magic?," Wicca Living, November 6, 2017, https://wiccaliving.com/what-is-magic/.

Mysticism, or magic, is a practice and belief that was developed and passed down from traditional paganism. It involves individuals who were committed to studying themselves, this inner work often occurred in isolation for a deeper expansion. Mystics – including Wiccans, Druids, and pagans – use spells, charms, incantations, and potions but they are not as dramatic or extreme and instantaneous as we may expect them to be. Mystics work with nature and the life cycle of the Earth to connect with the beings around them. The magic used and practiced within these religions and belief systems is a magic that is personal as the individual. Within mysticism, there are usually no quick spells to fix a broken object as we may see in a fantasy movie. For example, mystics may perform rituals or cast spells to better their fortune, to gain a promotion at work, or to help an ill loved one, has a time delay.

Ultimately, magic is the ability to looking within and connect with nature which allows you to have influence over and ultimately change or manipulate your reality.

As a result of the image of witchcraft that is presented to society in books, movies, and television, there are still a few points of contention and confusion that surround magic and witchcraft that mostly stem from the language we use.

We tend to use the same language to describe dark magic and the spectacle of magic that we use to describe true magic and the craft we find within ourselves. Thankfully there are some terms that we can replace with others to help clarify our meaning. For this reason, we have chosen – unless we are specifically mentioning one historical use or philosophy of witchcraft – to replace the word witch with mystic as the term 'witch' has a negative connotation. Think of what image pops in your head when you think of the term 'witch.' You either may be thinking of a green-skinned, pointy hat-headed character or thinking about how you may have called someone that as a slur. Using the word mystic, however, allows for a broader definition for several reasons. First, it relates to truth-seekers and searchers of knowledge. Second, it helps us to understand that someone can work alongside the energy of nature without using this power in malevolent ways. Furthermore, the mystic journey is one that is open to discovering more about themselves and their innate power. Therefore, there will be a conscious effort to change the language we use for the rest of the book, to help bring a more positive connotation to the practice of magic.

Magic is a much more subtle and humble practice than we are originally led to believe, based on the images of magic portrayed within society and different pop culture fads. Individuals are not simply born with the ability to perform magic nor are they naturally experts in the field. Rather individuals must learn and practice to perfect this ability.

If we look at the pagan definition of magic, we can see similar trends form. Individuals who are familiar with magic from a young age and not completely pulled away by the distractions of our society usually have families that practice a specific kind of magic. Similar to fictional magic, some individuals choose to explore their abilities on their own. This is not entirely unheard of, although it can sometimes be challenging to perfect your craft without the support of a community.

You must remember what we are trying to explore and help you understand this version of pagan magic; not the magic that we see in books, films, and television. The similarities made above are merely made to show that fictional magic is itself based on something real and very true within our world and is simply exaggerated for entertainment.

CHAPTER 2

Ancient Magic: Animism

At its most basic definition, Animism is the belief there is a supernatural power and force that flows through all objects. This power binds all individuals and things as all things in nature are alive. This magic is developed through the communication and connection with this natural force in our world.

In some circles, Animism is considered to be the first mystical practices throughout the world. While Animism is not well known, portions of Animism are embedded into other sects such as Shintoism, Panentheist religions, Hinduism, and Buddhism. Rather than focusing on doctrine and proper adherence to rules, Animism – and the other sects like it – follow more of a code of ethics cultivated from deep respect and appreciation for the world around them and how it nurtures human life. Furthermore, these sects pay reverence to many gods, rather than just one all-powerful one.

History of Animism

It was in the late 19th century that the term 'Animism' came to be coined by Sir Edward Taylor. Taylor studied Native American teachings and found that the belief of souls and energies connected all things in the world to be present. However while the term 'Animism' is more modern, Animism is a far more ancient sect. Animism is a historical and traditional belief system held by many Native Americans and Aboriginals. To Native Americans and Aboriginals, everything in nature is alive and has a spirit. Out of the respect and reverence Aboriginal people have for the land and animals in our world, over time nature revealed great secrets about this world to them – much of which remains hidden to this day – as Aboriginals have fiercely protected the secrets of this powerful magic. Before we begin into the specific understanding of Animism it is important to note that it is not to be considered a religion. Rather, it is a belief system that people follow by communicating with nature and their world. It is this collective power that provides value, purpose and guidance to their lives.[1]

In sum, Animism focuses on the idea of oneness with the world. Reflecting this belief, Animists encourage individuals to cultivate their relationship in harmony with the world and help them to understand how we are all connected in this world.

Traditions and Rituals Within Animism

Telepathy and Second Sight

The phenomena of telepathy and second sight are the ability to be able to sense something or communicate beyond our five senses.

---

[1] "Animism," Animism - an overview | ScienceDirect Topics, accessed October 8, 2021, https://www.sciencedirect.com/topics/social-sciences/Animism.

In Animism, these abilities were often considered to be closely linked to animals. Have you ever noticed that your dog is already waiting for you at the door when you come home as if they sensed you were on your way? Beyond this example, however, there have been many studies and recorded occurrences of animals being able to sense the coming or presence of something that humans do not sense. Dogs are said to be able to sense deceased spirits in a home, or even smell cancerous formations within a human.

Moving to wild animals, researchers have found that animals behave differently and change their demeanor before a large storm and farm animals begin to act more agitated a few days before a large harvest. The reason for this is said to be because the animals can sense that the storm or the day of butchery is coming. Of course, these abilities are largely due to their heightened senses, yet for the Animist these heightened senses are a way to connect with the world beyond the physical one. The belief is that animals have their own natural spirit and therefore able to recognize and understand subtle changes in their environment.

For Animism, this ability held by animals is not only revered but practiced. Animists see animals as communicators with other realms, spirits, and ancestors so Animists attempt to cultivate the same skills as the animal through a deep meditative state and identifying the animal which best suits their need or pursuit. To do so, they perform different rituals that include burning certain herbs around animals to encourage this communication and animals would often give them visions of land and hunting techniques.

Sweat Ceremonies[2]

Sweat ceremonies and lodges are important aspects of Animism. Sweating was seen as a way of purifying the body of illness, evil spirits, and anything harmful to the person. Therefore, lodges were built to encourage and facilitate sweating. A typical lodge would include a type of heat source such as hot stones and specially prepared herbs that increased the temperature to promote intense sweating. Many sweat lodges were built close to a body of water so the individual was able to cleanse after the ceremony and welcome the healing power from freshwater.

Usually made out of natural materials, the sweat lodge was a sacred place for many reasons. Depending on the reason and specific ceremony, either an individual would enter into the sweat lodge alone, or in a small group of people. If the individual was ill or had an evil spirit within their body, they would enter the sweat lodge alone and go through a personal and private ritual to remove the illness and spirit. Of course, if the individual was too ill or if the spirit was making the individual aggressive in some way then experienced members from the community would enter the ritual with them to ensure the patient's safety.

Sweat lodges were used to encourage and activate a relationship between man and higher spirits. While the individual sweats they repeatedly chant through prayer or song giving thanks to Mother

---

[2] Habits and Customs, accessed October 20, 2021, http://rimstead-cours.espaceweb. usherbrooke.ca/ANG4562/site/page%203.htm.

Earth. The action strengthens their spirituality and connection with the creator.

While the sweat ceremony can be performed for one person, it can also be performed for the whole community. If there is any type of illness that plagues the entire community then each member will also participate to heal the entire community.

Ceremony of Dreamtime[3]

For many of these ancient kinds of magic, nothing was written down in order to protect the teachings and instead was transmitted orally from generation to generation. However, some mystical practices have to be experienced instead of being taught. For this reason, the Dreamtime ceremony is used.

For those who follow Animism, dreams show the connection between an individual and the spirit world. Within this belief, visions are not simply images that are shown to us, but instead a way of connecting with the spirits of the world and the ancestors. Receiving and interpreting signs from spirits can be difficult in our waking life as there are plenty of distractions keeping us from noticing these signs. However, when we dream, we have no such distractions so Animists spend time interpreting their dreams. In some Dreamtime ceremonies, certain substances are ingested by the individual to help clear their mind and to help their dreams become more lucid.

---

[3] "Australian Aboriginal Ceremony," Aboriginal Incursions, accessed October 20, 2021, https://aboriginalincursions.com.au/the-dreaming/aboriginal-ceremony-explained.

Essentially, a Dreamtime ceremony is a specific and strategic sleep that the individual undergoes to try and discern meaning from their dreams. In this Dreamtime state, the individual comes to a primordial communication with a spirit that they are incapable of doing so in the waking world. As a result, our mind can flow freely among the realm of the non-physical. It has been said that individuals who undergo a Dreamtime ceremony have been able to glimpse into the future as their mind is no longer limited by the physical nature of time and space.

Similar to meditation, Dreamtime ceremonies can help individuals heal and solve a specific problem as the dream provides their solution. Dreamtime ceremonies are purposeful induced sleep-like states that can lead to the individual coming in contact with their ancestors and the spiritual realms to discern meaning from their dreams.

The Pipe Ceremony[4]

The pipe ceremony is a ritual and tradition that is sacred among many indigenous and aboriginal cultures, and to Animism as well. It is a process that facilitates the connection and communication between our reality and the spiritual realms.

It is said that it is the smoke that is created by the individual and is pushed into the air and reaches the upper world as a result. "Nothing is more sacred. The pipe is our prayers in physical form. Smoke becomes our words; it goes out, touches everything, and becomes a

---

4 "The Native American," Native American Pipe Ceremony, accessed October 13, 2021, http://www.native-americans-online.com/native-american-pipe-ceremony.html.

part of all there is. The fire in the pipe is the same fire in the sun, which is the source of life."[5] Moreover, because natural substances are used to burn and create smoke, the pipe ceremony is a way of connecting and unleashing intention into the natural world.

Just as different spells and incantations are used depending on the intention, a different pipe and pipe ceremony is selected to suit the type of communication and spirit the individual is trying to facilitate. There are many aspects of the pipe ceremony that can differ depending on the situation, like the pipe, the tobacco, and the actual ceremony.

However, there are some commonalities between all of the different pipe ceremonies. Almost every ceremony includes multiple participants and includes a similar reason to be performed which allows for bonds and connections to be formed between individuals. It is said that if you are invited to a pipe ceremony, your relationship with this person will be strengthened.

Ancestor Work[6]

Ancestors are highly revered amongst animists. Ancestors can either be your family members (blood ancestors) or members of your culture, religion, or community (spiritual ancestors). Without our

---

[5] Ibid.

[6] John Beckett, "Ancestor Work," John Beckett (Patheos Explore the world's faith through different perspectives on religion and spirituality! Patheos has the views of the prevalent religions and spiritualities of the world., April 14, 2021), https://www.patheos.com/blogs/johnbeckett/2021/04/ancestor-work.html.

ancestors, we would not be here nor would our society be as developed without those generations that came before us.

Many individuals who follow and practice Animism understand our ancestors had a great influence on the world we live in. It is those who have gone before us who conquered challenges and struggles for us to live in the society that we do today. There is an understanding among Animists that we owe a debt of appreciation and reverence for those ancestors.

Animists believe that the spirits of our ancestors are present within the land around us so participating in rituals and traditions that honor the land and show appreciation for the natural world is a type of gratitude to our ancestors. That being said, it is incredibly important to note that the invoking of ancestors and any human spirit should be reserved for only the most seasoned and experienced mystic and Animist. Modern-day Animists are not forced to show appreciation to those ancestors who were known to be harmful, evil, or abusive of other people or the land. If a specific ancestor was known to be malevolent or abusive in any way, they were purposefully never spoken of or acknowledged again.

The ancestors are more than just the history of our society and our lineage. They are present in our lives and are presented and represented in the world through nature. Therefore, ancestor work in Animism refers to any ritual or practice that is specifically meant to honor, give thanks to, or allow ancestral knowledge to surface within them.

What Does Animism Have To Do With Magic?

Animism is considered to be the first belief system and way of life as it was strongly practiced and followed by indigenous cultures. Animism is more akin to a way of life that encourages the connection to the spirits of the earth and teaches its followers how to develop power based on these connections.

Animism is not formally a type of mysticism or witchcraft but rather a type of lorecraft. Lorecraft is the working of magic or energy within the realm of this dimension passed down by ancestors. The craft is used to protect, give gratitude, and respect the natural world around us. However, this doesn't mean that Animism is removed from witchcraft entirely since witchcraft is the working of magic by invoking spirits, natural or otherwise. Rather many practice a sort of magic in our modern-day that employ beliefs and traditions of Animism without even knowing it. As the types of crafts that were developed and have been derived from paganism call on the energies of nature, so do those who practice elements of Animism. For example Wiccans, Druids, and even neo-pagans focus on the energy of different natural elements and look for signs in that energy.

Furthermore, since this type of magic and personal craft encourages you to find your type of magical power, incorporating aspects of Animism into your practice can help to personalize it.

Through an exploration of Druidism, Wiccanism, and Animism, we can see that while each sect has roots based on the natural world they differ in the belief and religious systems that bring about this magic. Each of these different ancient magic types has its own community where individuals congregate, practice, and learn how to develop the different magical powers held within these different belief systems.

What is important to keep in mind as you move forward with your exploration is that this book is meant to present and introduce you to a world that you otherwise would have never explored. We understand that perhaps you may be entering into the magical community blind and unaware of what is available to you which makes the journey an intimidating one. For this reason, we implore you to take your time to fully understand the magnitude of opening gateways into other realms as undoing this action is not easy. We suggest that you perform your own research, look into your family history, and reach out to the different magical communities in your area to fully understand the force that is flowing through you and the responsibility of using it with integrity. Your gut feeling for whatever practice speaks to your heart is always the one to trust.

Moreover, keep an open mind to all possibilities as you move forward, not only through the book but through your life journey as well. While you can base your magical craft on one of the above schools, it is important to not hold steadfast to one over the other. From this point on, you will be taught how to form your own craft and personal magical practice that is free from the constraints of religions, other belief systems, and knowledge types. With the introductory knowledge given to you through this book, combined with a dedicated practice to learn all you can about nature and your natural home, you will be able to cultivate a craft more powerful than you ever thought possible.

CHAPTER 3

Ancient Magic: Druidism

Druids are individuals who have learned and developed their own magical abilities by drawing their power from the natural world. Druidism has developed into two schools of thought: ancient and modern Druidism. Ancient Druidism was seen as magic largely used for personal reasons. However, due to the development of Christianity, Druidism was changed and manipulated by opposing forces into a system that was closer to a religion that was deemed modern Druidism. Due to this change, many Druids were accepted as priests rather than wizards. The deep religious aspect of Druid magic came as it evolved and started its long journey to modern druidism.

It is important to understand the differences and similarities between the two schools and conceptualizations of magic in Druidism.

What is Ancient vs Modern Druidism

The word Druid comes from the Celtic word Doire which means oak tree or the idea of wisdom. As a result, Druid is often translated to wise oak or knower of the oak tree. Druidism began as a sort of spiritual group or tribe that concerned itself with the natural world that surrounded the power that could potentially be found within. The classical or ancient Druids believed that the strength and knowledge could be found in natural disasters and the natural progression of nature could be applied, and used by humans.

Dating back to 44 BC, this first conception of Druidism was largely a shamanic religion because it directs contact and communication with spirits and the use of holistic medicines found in nature. Through this lens, we can see how it is closely related to Animism as both spiritual practices deal with communication with spirits and reliance on the natural world for medicinal and spiritual resources.

Unfortunately, the ancient Celts did not necessarily write anything down as sacred knowledge was passed down to a select few. The full extent of these teachings took twenty to thirty years before training was complete. What is recorded is solely the interpretation by Christian Romans and such recordings are tainted because any alternative belief system was seen as heresy.

As Christianity began to grow in Western Europe it systematically pushed aside and made little room for any contrary or pagan beliefs. By the 17th and 18th centuries, any sign of a pagan religion was rather scarce except Druidism. Since many Druid 'holy' dates coincided with the holy dates of Christianity, Druidism was taken under the wing of Christianity and became a sort of hybrid religion of that time. What helped this assimilation was Julius Caesar.

Julius Caesar championed the Roman Empire for two very influential years from 46-44 BCE. During this time, he wrote extensively about the religious power of Druidism when it was in its traditional stages. Caesar enlisted the help of Druids to walk the battlefields and spread the word of religion and bring about peace. Druids became advisors to kings and political leaders to help not only spread the word of religion but to help with different political issues as well.

As a result, Christian priests found that Druidism was not as threatening as the other pagan religions. Christian priests did this in an attempt to not only strengthen their own religion but to control Druidism. After all, if Christianity took over and subsumed the followers of Druidism then it would never become a threat to Christianity like the other pagan religions were proving to be.[1]

Modern Druidism kept many of the same beliefs of its traditional version while some critical aspects changed. Druids were seen as priestly figures in the community who worked through the church rather than the political aides. There began to be a sense of divine worship to the Druids' belief systems. Druids also began to enjoy the same privileges as Christian priests and were given much of the same reverence. They were seen as figures of authority and given the power to perform their rituals within the community and were even given permission to hand down punishments and judgments in certain situations.[2]

---

[1] "Druids," Myths Encyclopedia, accessed October 8, 2021, http://www.mythencyclopedia.com/Dr-Fi/Druids.html.
[2] "Lesson Two ~ Druids Ancient and Modern," The Druid Network, accessed February 21, 2022, https://druidnetwork.org/what-is-druidry/learning-resources/polytheist/lesson-two/.

This modern and religious version of Druidism is what is practiced currently.

Traditions and Rituals Within Druidism

Although Druidism changed its conception and acceptance, many of the basic beliefs and rituals stayed the same over time. Specifically, Druidism is separated into three legs: immortality, rituals, and omens.

Immortality

Druids believe that the soul is immortal and can be reincarnated. They believe that life flows in an infinite cycle and this infinite cycles allows the Druids to believe that their souls will follow a similar pattern. As a result, the Druids do not fear death the same way that other religions do.

Rituals[3]

Many rituals are important in Druidism and are usually performed on the same day every year and in the same way. Moreover, these rituals are nearly always connected to whatever part of the life or seasonal cycle that is happening presently. Many Druid holy days are also significant in the secular calendar. There are said to be 8 holy days in Druidism:

---

[3] "The Wheel of the Year in the Druid Tradition – Description of Druidic Holidays," The Druid's Garden, August 12, 2016, https://druidgarden.word-press.com/2013/04/06/the-wheel-of-the-year-in-the-druid-tradition-description-of-druidic-holidays/.

Samhain

Samhain falls on October 31. On this day, the Druids believe that life and death are the closest they will ever be as Samhain stands between the last day of the harvest and the beginning of winter.

Yule

Alban Arthan is the winter solstice and is celebrated on December 21. During the winter months, many natural elements go through their seasonal death cycle to preserve themselves in the cold. Druids will wait outside for the sunrise as this symbolizes that even on the darkest day there will be light and rebirth.

Imbolc

Usually falling on the first or second of February, this holy day recognizes and celebrates motherhood. The celebration of motherhood on this day represents that the world's seasonal rebirth is coming soon.

Alban Eiler

Falling on March 21, this holiday is also known as the first day of spring. This holy day is the full realization of spring and rebirth and is representative of balance as the day is equally light and dark.

Beltane

Happening around May 1, this holy day is representative of fertility. Now that the rebirth of the world is complete and the land has come back to life from winter, the land is now fertile once more.

Alban Hefin

This holy day is the Summer Solstice (otherwise known as the first day of summer) and is meant to celebrate the nowness of the moment. During this day, the Druids celebrate their lives and freedom in their lives.

Lughnasadh

Druids celebrate the fire festival of Lughnasadh on August 1. It marks the first day of the harvest. Druids celebrate abundance on this day and appreciate the bountiful harvest that is to come in the following months.

Alban Elfed

Celebrated usually around September 21, this holy day is one where Druids push for recognition of balance in the life cycle. As the world begins to cool, the Druids begin to recognize the darker months and days are on their way and they celebrate the balance that allows for their yearly cycle to be continued again the following year and the continuous cycle that allows for their souls to be reincarnated.

Omens

Omens are also an important part of the Druid belief system. These are the signs that the Druids read and the spirits that they communicate with to yield foresight. Without the omens that represent spiritual communication, the Druid rituals would go unanswered. Therefore, the Druid must be able to read the omens and signs presented to them for them to fully realize the power of the natural world around them.

Druidism is only one more example of how pagan belief systems, mysticisms, and religions have developed over time. Just as Druidism has close ties to Animism, concepts found in Druidism have since been developed for more modern interpretations and mystic beliefs.

CHAPTER 4

Ancient Magick: Wicca

Another instantiation of magick with a 'k' is Wiccanism. Generally speaking, Wiccanism, or as it is known by some neo-paganism, is a Western and Europe-based magickal movement that includes followers from England and Scotland. In modern-day society, the word Wicca – thanks in part to the ubiquitous and incorrect use of the term – is often synonymous with witches. Wiccanism has a history that spans hundreds of years and challenges the very stereotypes that it is given today. Through the exploration of the history of Wiccans, we can understand what this system of magick entails.

History of Wiccanism

Unlike Animism and Druidism, Wiccanism is a modern religion created out of the intention to move away from Druidism. Gerald Gardner (1884-1964) is said to have started Wiccanism in Great Britain and is considered the 'father of modern witchcraft.' Gardner's book Witchcraft Today first used the term Wicca which he defined to mean a wise person. The book was supposedly based on the insight he revived from a horned god, after a chance encounter in the forest. Gardner also wrote and published a collection of spells and rituals that would be used at that time and beyond to help underscore the philosophy of the mystical belief system.[1]

Gardner was a practicing Druid but through his travels, he became distant from the practice and quite interested in the teachings of the practicing occultist Aleister Crowley. Gardner began to explore the beliefs as presented by Crawley and also took great interest in teaching of Freemasonry too. This exploration was the catalyst from Druidism towards something else entirely.

What pushed Gardner over the edge was the 'us versus them' environment that was developed in society at the time. Christianity was working to instill a sort of separation within society. If we are left alone with any sort of belief system human beings would seek out only four basic needs: food, shelter, social contact, and free choice. What Christianity was trying to do was to create an existential space between each individual. By labeling members of society as either Christians - us- or the non-religious- them- the leaders of the church encouraged a sense of segregation within the community. As human beings want and yearn for social contact the church was hoping to bring more followers under their umbrella as they would not want to be considered as an outsider or a 'them', but rather be a member of the community or an 'us'.

---

[1] History.com Editors, "Wicca," History.com (A&E Television Networks, March 23, 2018), https://www.history.com/topics/religion/wicca.

Druidism followed much the same tactics that Christianity employed and Wiccanism was an option for those members of society who had been named the outsiders to form a different community. Thus Wiccanism was officially born.[2]

Wiccanism made its way to North America during the 1960s. As soon as it hit American shores, it took off and began to spread quickly thanks to the counter-culture revolution, which mirrored Wiccan traits. As a result, Wiccanism became known not only as a neo-pagan religion but also as an environmental and feminist movement.

Even with its popularity, however, it would be another twenty years until Wiccanism was recognized by the government to be a religion. What legitimizing the religion did do, however, was make it even more popular.

Traditions and Rituals Within Wiccanism

The first belief that is important to Wiccan is what is known as the Wiccan Rede. The Wiccan Rede is a poem that provides the Wiccan follower with advice. There are many lines of the poem that are important but the most important line is "That it Harm None, Do as thou Wilt."[3] This phrase means that as long as it harms no one then the action can be done. This phrase is important as it helps to emphasize that Wiccans do not intend to cause harm to anyone.

---

[2] https://www.bbc.co.uk/religion/religions/paganism/subdivisions/wicca.shtml
[3] Ibid.

Initiation Rituals

There are also initiation rituals that are involved with Wiccanism. These initiations are personal and secret rituals that are meant to mark the time and place when you begin your journey into this magickal practice. Each individual who goes through the ritual makes a vow dedicating themselves to their practice. Other than that common element, it is said that the rituals can involve whatever the person chooses. It is meant to be a moment where you leave your old self behind and take an oath to a new way of life.

Covens

Another important aspect of Wiccanism is the idea of covens. A coven, also known as a circle, is a group of individuals who practice the magick of Wiccans. Some covens are created with a specific purpose in mind; for instance, they can be created for a short amount of time to achieve one goal or one long-term spell, or they can be created for a lifetime. No matter how long the coven is together, it is usually a group of Wiccans who have similar philosophies and methods of practice and look to the coven for support and community. Additionally, you do not need to stick with just one coven. You can be part of multiple covens at once.

When you are exploring the magical and the mystical, you are opening yourself to dangers and anxieties and the coven provides you with the support to do so. While there are many benefits of practicing with a coven, you do not have to as it is up to the individual mystic. No matter the outcome, each mystic ultimately walks this path alone.

Worshipping Two Gods

There are generally two gods in the Wiccan religion: the Triple Goddess and the Great Horned God.

The Triple Goddess

This goddess is named as such as she is seen as a maiden, a mother, and a crone. Each of these faces represents one part of the life cycle with the maiden representing youth, seduction, and innocence; the mother showing fertility and nurturing power, and the crone encompassing death and dying and wisdom and knowledge. Ultimately this goddess represents the earth and the powerful yet nurturing and giving sense of the earth.

The Great Horned God

The Great Horned God, on the other hand, is largely associated with the wild side of nature. This god is seen to represent the wild animals that roam the earth, the notion of survival, the strength needed to do so, and, ultimately, the primal and instinctive side of living in nature.

Together these two gods allow for the balance between both sides of nature and the two sides that make up Wiccanism.

8 Holy Days

There are 8 holy days in Wiccanism that are similar to those that are found in Druidism. Similarly, these holy days represent the changes in the outer environment that happen with the change in seasons and how those changes are mirrored and effective in humans.

More specifically, Wiccans recognize four specific days out of these eight: the new moon, the vernal equinox, summer solstice, and Halloween. These days in particular are powerful for the practicing Wiccan as nature's energy is concentrated and flowing freely. To help boost their magickal powers, Wiccans prefer to be known as witches and will utilize additional tools in their practice such as cauldrons, wands, cloaks and altars to invoke spirits, deities and perform rituals. Wiccans also maintain a log of spells known as a shadow book.

The Practice of Magick

To Wiccans, magick is a powerful influence over the world around us as it is a power that comes from within the individual with the help of the deities and can be strengthened and weakened based on the holy day and time of the year. Magick, for the Wicca, is practiced through very specific rituals used routinely over the year.

Ultimately, Wiccanism, while being one of the newest sects developed from paganism, still holds and employs many of the same core beliefs of its father sect, while modernizing the rituals as time moves on to still be relevant for the twentieth and twenty- first centuries.

CHAPTER 5

The Other Realms

A common thread that has been seen throughout the exploration of paganism, Druidism, Wiccanism, and Animism, is that its possible to communicate with other worlds. This practice is a personal choice but isn't necessary to work magic in your reality.

These otherworldly dimensions are not usually seen or experienced by the common man or woman because these worlds are not necessarily ones that we can simply walk into. Rather, they are conceptualized as different frequencies of time, space, and energies within with different kinds of beings and powers are used.

To briefly bring the term dimension out of the magical world for a moment, a dimension is commonly defined as a designated area or space that some things – either objects or beings – take up and inhabit. Mathematically, a dimension is designated by numbers, symbols, and coordinates. However, and bringing the definition back to the subject at hand, dimensions in the magical realms are designated slightly differently.

While they are still areas that are designated by beings and things that take up space, these dimensions are not necessarily defined by coordinates because these dimensions are not seen or directly experienced by us. Rather they are considered to be dimensions as in other worlds that are separate to our own world and connection can only be accessed through your consent.

Pagans believe that there are three worlds: the Upper World, the Middle World, and the Lower World. We will discuss them in more detail below:

Upper World

The first world and dimension to explore are the Upper World. This world is usually considered to be the world of the divine where highly evolved gods, angels, guardians, and some spirits live.

Usually seen positively, the Upper World resides above our reality at a higher frequency and protectively looks down upon the other worlds and dimensions.

While the Upper World is not usually accessible for the common man, communication between the Upper World and other realms is possible. Such communication is commonly referred to as intervention as the more powerful and influential world – the Upper – is imposing its power on another. Moreover, due to the Upper World being beyond our tangible world, there is a fantastical and enchanting element to it which leads to the idea that any communication with the Upper World is fantastical as well.

Middle World

The Middle World is conceptualized as lying beneath the upper one: it 'sits' between the Upper and the Lower Worlds. The Middle World is our reality and where humans, animals, plants, and all other tangible and physical items we hold dear live.

This does not mean that the Middle World does not have magical power within. Instead, the magic found within the borders of our world is practical and useful to those who live within it. As modern mystics, you will learn to pull your power from this world and nature around you rather than trying to pull it from a world that is beyond you.

The physical setup of the world mirrors the ethical and moral aspects of our world as well. Every human is sandwiched between doing what is right and what is wrong. As a modern mystic, you too are placed between good and evil to ultimately choose your fate. As you explore and begin your journey exploring your internal mysticism, you must be careful to not fall more one way or another. You must use your powers to create balance for good and personal reasons. You have to resist the urge to develop a strong power for selfish reasons, yet not be afraid to use your power to better your own life as the Middle World is all about manifesting and experiencing the physical and emotional reality we desire. Therefore, the Middle World is not only the realm in which we live and derive but it also represents the balance that must be practiced when developing your mysticism.

Lower World

The Lower World in the world that sits below the Middle World and it is where malevolent energies and spirits reside. Elements like evil spirits and demons stay within the Lower World and look up to examine the Middle World for gateways into our physical realm. The Lower World seeks to influence our reality through intervention and desire.

Since this world is seen as malevolent, it is considered to be the origin of temptation, desire, and impulse. While these can be motivating factors, they can also lead to selfishness, narcissism, general immorality, and unethical behavior.

The idea of different worlds is not only a pagan ideology. Many, if not all religions have a sort of three-fold or multi-world structure to their belief systems. Perhaps the most well known one is found in Christianity. For Christians, the Upper World is Heaven, the Middle World is Earth, and the Lower World is Hell.

While we can call upon the other realms for inspiration and intervention, when it comes to the modern mystic and developing your own magical power from within yourself, we must stay within our designated realm. Any venture into the other realms can prove to be challenging even for most experienced mystic. Before any new mystics begin their journey they have to understand this concept fully. Although there is magic in every realm, there is danger in relying heavily on and exploring the powers of the Upper and Lower Worlds. Although these worlds are no more powerful than the Middle World they provide a kind of allure or curiosity that distracts from the magic within us. The modern mystic explores their powers by developing them internally and expressing them externally and if we continuously reach for powers from the Upper and Lower Worlds, we are doing the opposite as we are exploring powers beyond ourselves and trying to control them.

Calling on divine and mystical intervention from these other worlds reduces personal power. Instead, it pushes the individual to reach out for help, rather than to look within themselves to find it. If someone consistently reaches to the Lower World for their mystical powers, they become the personification of the 'witch' stereotype which bring a malevolent connotation to the practicing mystic.

As a new mystic these concepts might be hard to grasp. We can look to scientific world for examples that reflect these energetic frequencies. The human eye cannot see all light waves because there are a variety of alternative in the light frequency spectrum. However, scientists have developed devices to prove that these light waves are indeed present in our existence even if we cannot see them explicitly. In the same way, while we cannot 'see' the other realms through the development of your magical powers, we are shown that they are present.

It should also be noted that we could also demonstrate this point through the explanation of sound waves. There are sounds we can hear that travel at a medium frequency which indicates our Middle World. Then there are higher frequency sounds and lower frequency sounds that we cannot hear with the human sense of sound. Each indicates and represents the Upper and Lower Worlds respectively. Understanding the realms in this way can also lend itself to understanding why animals are so revered and held sacred in the different mystic systems and religions. For example, since animals can hear these higher pitched sounds they are, through the eyes of the mystics, able to communicate with the higher realm.

When it comes to developing and exploring your mystical powers it is important to understand how the three realms work together and communicate with each other and use that as inspiration only to practice your mysticism. You want to ensure that you stay within your realm to not lose control over or trade your powers to ensure a stronger mystical practice.

CHAPTER 6

Universal Law And The Nature of Reality

"The Principles of Truth are Seven; he who knows these, understandingly, possesses the Magic Key before whose touch all the Doors of the Temple fly open... He who grasps the truth of the Mental Nature of the Universe is well advanced on The Path to Mastery."

— *The Kybalion*

While magic is largely used to alter the world around us it also is bound by the natural laws of the realm. We have seen through the exploration of paganism that three of the mystical belief systems and religions that came from paganism – Animism, Druidism, and Wiccanism – have their own beliefs and rituals to manipulate the events around them.

Laws of the universe govern how our world works and are unique only to the Middle World. The universe is a spiraling vortex expanding and contracting into balance, it knows no wrong or right but only balance and constant evolution forward. These natural laws give balance to our world and provide an operating structure.[1] When we employ these natural laws and work with them in our craft we work in harmony with the magical flow of the universe.

Ultimately, many use science as a base to understand their own mystical powers and demystify the practice of magic.

It is encouraged that practicing mystics are aware of these laws of nature and to not work against them as working against these powerful laws raises the risk of hitting some challenges and roadblocks while developing your craft. To consider it another way, if we break laws we get into some trouble and we are unable to move ahead as an individual in society. Fines, jail time, and removal of societal privileges are all consequences that can hurt or temporarily affect our development as a member of society. If we break or go against the natural laws then it will disrupt your development with added consequences that you may not fully be aware of yet.

Before we explore the different types of universal laws, we must first understand the idea of mutable and immutable laws so we can better understand how these universal laws affect us. Mutable laws are those that can change our reality directly. We can apply the laws to our lives as we see fit and even manipulate them at certain times. Immutable laws, on the other hand, are eternal and universal. They are always being applied and remain present in our lives. We cannot move

---

[1] Jessica Estrada, "How to Harness the Power of the 12 Laws of the Universe to Improve Your Life," Well+Good, August 27, 2021, https://www.welland-good.com/laws-of-the-universe/#:~:text=Law%20of%20divine%20one-ness&text=%E2%80%9CThis%20law%20states%20that%20we,the%20collec-tive%E2%80%94not%20just%20ourselves.

beyond immutable laws. With this understanding, we will discuss some of the natural laws that govern our world:

Law of Divine Oneness

The law of divine oneness is considered the first law of nature because the other laws of reality are predicated on it. It refers to the idea that we, as humans, are related to all other things in the world and that all other things in the world are interconnected.

Every person and thing in our reality is made of atoms and, as a result, means that everything we do is connected by a force and can affect all other things.

To work with this law is to understand that everything we do will affect you and then someone or something else. Having kinship with these consequences can help us become intuitive to how we can bring about certain consequences and manipulate our reality.

Law of Correspondence

The law of correspondence states that our lives are built on the pieces of our day to day routine. Humans are creatures of habit. What we do daily comforts us and builds our lives, relationships, and beliefs. Due to this comfort, we may be blinded to their potential detrimental consequences. Slouching may be comfortable but it can lead to more serious health issues. A daily routine of continuously working non-stop may become comfortable to us but it is damaging as we can be ignoring or neglecting other parts of our lives that are just as important.

Therefore, to work with this law, we must evaluate these patterns and habits and pay attention to their consequences and how they make us feel. This law is not meant to discourage us. Rather, it is meant to encourage us to find those patterns and habits that are productive, add benefit to our lives in order to bring about the best version of ourselves, and, in turn, allow us to develop our inner strength and power.

Law of Intent

Also known as the law of inspired action, this law of reality states that our intention for what we want our actions to do and say about us is strictly in our minds. Therefore, it is up to us to ensure that our actions match our intentions. When we act in accordance with our intentions, we supercharge the action and set in motion the motivation and action to inspire the results of what we desire.

To work with this law we must try our hardest to ensure that our intentions and desires are aligned with our actions and voiced into existence, as this force will bring about a stronger and more purposeful practice.

Law of Cause and Effect

The law of cause and effect means that with every situation, event, or action, there is a cause and an effect. In other words, there is always something that brought about an action or event, and there is always going to be a result or a consequence of that action. It is important to note that the cause and effect are rarely one thing. Rather, one cause can have a series of effects that grow from moment to moment.

Many mystics understand this law as Karma, or, in colloqueal terms, "what goes around comes around." To ensure that you are keeping in line with this law it is important to be aware of the possible consequences of our actions and act in such a way to encourage certain desired effects. Fully understand what is meant by 'harm' as there are many different interpretations of this. Kind actions breed kind consequences and hurtful actions breed harmful consequences. As you only have control of yourself it is best to focus your craft inward and not on others as to interfere with the 'free will' of another person is considered very harmful.

Law of Belief

This law goes against what we are frequently told in our reality. In order for something to be real we have to see it. If this statement were true then our knowledge, as humans, would be limited to only what we have seen with our own eyes. Understanding that there are truths and aspects of our reality that we perhaps may not be able to experience allows us to be open to the world around us and open to our potential to influence the world around us. Be sure to be critical of your beliefs and try not to be fooled into believing only what your eyes can see or nurturing the belief or doctrines of others groups.

This law is incredibly important when it comes to the practice of magic as the energy that will feed your magical endeavors ultimately come from the non-physical world. A mystic has to understand their energy to be powerful. Furthermore, when it comes to formulating a personal craft the key to success is that whatever you believe to be true for long enough will become your reality. You have the absolute power to choose your destiny and you simply need to believe in the power that resides within you in order to ignite it.

Law of Compensation

Compensation is the idea that we will be paid for our endeavours. This is usually seen and understood in terms of employment and labor. The law of compensation expands to include compensation for our spiritual and non-employment based work. Our actions of kindness, generosity, humility, and sacrifice will be compensated by a higher power and by the cycle of nature.

It is important to remember that our compensation may not present itself clearly or in a form that we expected it to. If we go in with the expectation to be compensated with a verbal thank you from a specific person, we may not receive it as such. Rather we may receive compensation by someone else being kind to us. No matter the kind of compensation, it is expected that we are always compensated in some way for our actions.

Therefore to work in alignment with this law we must be open and accepting of all forms of compensation and be grateful for any instances of it. We must try to let go of our expectations and be grateful for the compensation we do get.

Law of Mentalism

The law of mentalism is an immutable law, it states that the world exists in our minds before it exists outside of us. The law goes on to say that the world continues to live and exist in our minds, even if aspects of our world perish.

This law goes hand in hand with the law of belief as it allows for the acceptance of reality beyond what we can see. This law is important to understand as it encourages the mystic to focus on their mind and the intentions and desires held within the mind when they are trying to influence the world around them. Moreover, in focusing on the reality of the mind the mystic strengthens their inner power.

CHAPTER 7

The Law of Agreement

In the last chapter, we explored some of the natural laws that govern our world that we can work with to strengthen our inner power. That being said, some laws of our world have such a large impact on the development and use of magic and mysticism that they warrant their own chapter, one of which is the law of agreement. The law of agreement – both within and outside of the context of magic and mysticism – is rather complex and overwhelming to understand. For this reason, we will simplify the definition and implications here.

The Law of Agreement in General

We enter into so many agreements automatically in society today that the enormity behind such agreements has been lost in many cases. For this reason, we plan to reignite its power within this chapter. Outside of the world of magic and mysticism, the law of agreement states that entering into a contract or agreement with someone creates a sense of shared expectations and responsibilities that are enforceable based on the nature of the agreement.[1]

---

[1] "Contract," Legal Information Institute (Legal Information Institute), accessed

Entering into an agreement can range from simply entering into a relationship with someone to making a legally binding agreement. Most often when the law of agreement is used outside of the world of magic, it is used in the legal world which makes contracts able to be enforced by bodies of law. These are the kinds of agreements that many people are familiar with. But there are other more subtle agreements that individuals are not aware they are in.

In our everyday life, there are a variety of agreements that we enter into without realizing it as a formal agreement. We enter into agreements with our friends, our family members, our loved ones, and even strangers, and they enter into agreements with us for a variety of reasons as well. As such, entering into agreements with other individuals binds us and connects us to that other person.

While there are some agreements that are meant to last forever or for a long time – such as a marriage or a close friendship – there are others much more constrained. Say you go to a lender in search of applying and being accepted for a mortgage.[2] A mortgage is a kind of agreement that you enter into with a stranger that they will front you the money for your home and property under the promise and agreement that you will pay them back. Most people consider this exchange to be the most important agreement they'll make in a lifetime because they are aware of the agreed timeframe attached to it. As you can see there is a range of expectations and responsibilities

---

October 15, 2021, https://www.law.cornell.edu/wex/contract#:~:text=Definition,consideration%3B%20capacity%3B%20and%20legality.

[2] "Mortgage (n.)," Etymology, accessed October 15, 2021, https://www.etymonline.com/word/mortgage.

that are shared by both you and the lender. The expectation placed on you is that you will pay and honor the rate or return.

The expectation of the lender is that they will not change any details of the agreement without your knowledge, in addition to keeping track of the loan agreement to not allow you to over or underpay.

Interestingly, it is the signature that is the real magic here, the promise to generate the value each month is which brings the possibility into existence. The agreement will last as long as the terms dictate; in this case, specifically, a mortgage usually lasts until the end of the agreed time period or the individual passes. Interestingly the term mortgage literally means a pledge made until the individual is dead.

Even if you do not have a mortgage, you still enter into agreements many times over in your life, thereby binding and connecting you to many people. These are known as social agreements. There are certain behaviors that we do and do not do in public as a part of upholding our position as members of society. For instance, there is the agreement that humans choose to be governed by a select group of individuals and others to ensure protection and safety, one should not shout fire in a crowded place unless there is a fire or emergency.

An agreement is universally binding with anything from your word, your handshake, or your signature - so beware! While you will often know when entering into agreements there are more subtle situations where you may not.

While it may seem like you can make free choices, all of your choices and actions are bound within the limitations and confines of what is acceptable under the terms of the agreement. For example, let us say any institution /business for employment. Once you have signed the pages entering into the contract you must then abide by the terms of that contract. This can range from duties and responsibilities, holidays and the specific time you will work each day. Of course, agreeing to employment does not dictate the actions of your life, but it does dictate and restrict many of your daily actions and the amount of personal time you have to use. When you choose this type of relationship you bind yourself to the terms of that relationship. Likewise, even though you may not have fully understood the terms or language used, the agreement is binding nonetheless if your word or signature is present. Therefore you must understand the terms of every agreement before entering into it to be able to uphold your end of the relationship. Your institution will not care that you didn't understand the agreement when you entered it as they will expect you to uphold your end. It is important to fully understand the operations of this law in society, as the same philosophy apply with agreements in mysticism as these agreements are not only found in our secular society. Rather agreements must be understood as any oaths, rituals, gestures and are found in nearly every religion and belief system. In these contexts, the agreements we lock ourselves into are with its creators, spirits and deities found within the religion or ritual. The agreement is for worship and reverence in exchange for protection and help when asked for or called upon. However, do we really know this to be true without seeing the terms or knowing the original intent of those who created it, we are rather following the crowd and what has already been agreed in the past.[3]

The Law of Agreement And Mysticism

Understanding the law of agreement may be easy enough to understand, but understanding how it applies to the development of your mystical power is slightly more complicated. The complication comes from the nature and complexity of the agreements we enter into differ from our everyday life and our mystical life.

In our day-to-day lives the kinds of agreements that we enter into are – almost – always clear if we take the time to read and fully understand before signing. If the terms are not clear they can be made clear through a discussion with the other person. We can discuss the agreement expectations, or redefine the boundaries of our relationship with our friends, loved ones, and family. Even when we enter into agreements within a religious context the parameters of the agreement are made verbally by attendance or parental consent. Such communication is not necessarily accessible in the agreements we enter into mystically.

The agreements we enter in our mystic world and from the use of religions are oftentimes agreements with deities, ancestors, or unknown spirits. As a result, we are unable to directly ask them what exactly the terms of the agreement are and, sometimes, we are flying blind in the agreement. While our intention may be to honor every

---

[3] "The Law of Agreement," Bill Winston Ministries, accessed October 15, 2021, https://www.billwinston.org/The-Law-of-Agreement/.

agreement we enter into in our mystical world, we may accidentally abandon some of the responsibilities or expectations of the agreement over time. Unfortunately, agreements in the mystic realm are not as straightforward as those found in the social or financial world. This is why entering into agreements with other realms, spirits, deities is known as witchcraft and can be precarious and why magic must always be practiced with discernment and caution.

We are also more likely to enter into accidental agreements entirely when we deal with mystic powers. In our day-to-day lives, we confirm and give consent to our agreements through a handshake, verbal consent, or a signature but such confirmation is not guaranteed in the mystical world. We may not even know who we are agreeing with, endangering ourselves and our loved ones if we accidentally agree with a malevolent spirit or entity.

So how do we control and protect ourselves when it comes to the law of agreement and the mystical world? Perhaps the simplest way to be safe is to simply err on the side of caution. When you are beginning your journey into mysticism, it is best to assume that every time we cast a foreign spell – no matter if the spell is simply for protection, cleansing, or for a specific purpose – we are agreeing with a spirit or entity. Each time you cast a spell in the name of a specific spirit you are asking that spirit to help you bring about the desired result. If that specific result comes to be, you should consider that to be the spirit upholding its side of the agreement and it is on you to watch for that spirit to ask you to uphold your end of the agreement. Keep in mind that the more you ask of the spirit world, the higher the stakes and expectations will be for you.

For this reason, you should be cautious of the spells you cast. You should not be casting any spells for which you cannot reciprocate. To put it in words of our reality, you would not enter into a mortgage agreement if you were not able to pay back the loan.

Likewise, you should not enter into a mystical agreement if you are unable to repay that which you do not know.

This is why it is important to cast spells and practice magic based on your own intentions and not with a reference or in the name of a specific spirit. In using your intention and power you are not entering into a limited agreement with another spirit but freeing yourself of these contracts and agreements and strengthening your own powers. Do not get caught in the belief that you must call upon other spirits as such a practice is not required in the slightest.

Due to this law of agreement, it is highly suggested that when you begin your journey into your inner power and mysticism you stay within the confines of your own power and world and limit your requests of other spirits until you become skilled and have a better understanding of expectations. When you use your original intent, you set the laws of the agreement and relationship. When you use another's intent then there may be some aspects of the relationship that you do not want to abide by or that you do not know.

CHAPTER 8

Intention

As we move closer to learning how to cast spells and use our magical and mystical powers, we still must discuss the concept of Intention. Our intention is truly the source of all our power as it sets into motion the motivation and action necessary to manifest an aim or a goal that we have in mind.

Many of us have probably heard the word intention in two popular contexts. The first is the common definition of intention which means what we wish or aim to do. When we intend to do something, it means that we add action and desire to that action. If we do something unintentionally, it means that the results were not meant or anticipated to happen. Second, intention is also used frequently in yoga and meditation. Yogis set an intention before every routine and at the beginning of every day. In this context, the intention is a short phrase stating what they wish to accomplish that day. Intentions can be simple ("I wish you get through this entire routine without quitting") or they can be more complicated ("I will manifest and only think positive thoughts today").

Both of these contexts help to explain how the word is used within the magical and mystical world. While intention is what we want to bring in and accomplish in the world, it is also how we want to influence and affect the world around us. The intentions made with our mystic powers are akin to meditative mantras, affirmations, and prayers.

How Does Intention Work?

Everything in the world is made up of energy. Each object emits and absorbs energy consistently as part of its existence. Magic, therefore, is the ability to manipulate this energy as you will, and intentions work to bring about change as they physically change the energy surrounding us. When we speak, we are emitting an incredibly powerful force that affects all energies that flow around us. As we transmute thought energy into the physical world, it manifests to manipulate and influence the world around us.

There are generally two ways that intentions work using four universal laws. The first is based on the law of attraction, cause and effect, and oneness. When we speak out loud our intentions we are emitting the emotions and feelings that go along with the intention into the world as well. Therefore, when we speak positively and use corresponding words our bodies and selves emit positive energies and those positive energies will be returned to us. When we speak negatively our bodies and selves emit negative energies and negative energies will be returned to us. In this way, our intention is the source of our mysticism as it is closely linked to the kind of energies that we give and emit into the world.

The third way in which our intention is the source of our mysticism is through the law of vibration. The law of vibration is slightly more complex to understand as it has to do with the meaning of the words used to construct our intention. The vibrational patterns of words hold energy which vibrates at different levels of consciousness. To fully understand this second method of energy influence, we must trace this explanation back to sounds and letters. Sound is nothing but vibrations hitting and moving through the mechanism of our ears. The vibrations that are made when we speak are strong enough to move the energies in the world and influence even the solid material. For instance, strong sound vibrations can break and shatter glass, shake homes, and even be used to bounce small beads into delicate patterns. Moreover, every sound has the same sort of ability, particularly the words we choose to speak into existence. This leads us to the second part of how intentions influence our world: letters.

The twenty-six letters of our alphabet have been carefully designed and created to produce a specific sound when spoken. When we are taught the alphabet we are taught how to pronounce these sounds which make up the words we speak and hear. The specific combination of letters that form words produces a specific series of vibrations and the vibration of each word is different than any other word as long as it is spelled differently. Ultimately, the specific vibration pattern that is produced by the word then pushes up against the energies circulating our reality which in turn influences them. Interestingly, the method of ordering letters to create words is called *spelling* and the act of using these words and letters to push energies and vibrations throughout the world is known as spell casting. This is not a coincidence. In the same way that the spelling of each word dictates the vibration of sounds and meaning of the word, the spell that it casts dictates what the consequences will be.

Of course, we do not speak using simple words one at a time. Just as letters make up individual words, individual words make up sentences and ideas. Therefore a sentence, which is a specific combination of words, produces a very unique vibration sound pattern. Each unique sound pattern ultimately affects that which it is directed at, or in to contact with. Therefore the power of the intention is magnified by the law of vibration through the patterns of the words themselves.

While the specific order of letters and words creates different vibrations and energies, it is also amplified by how we say them that matters. This is where singing and chanting come in. Songs are words that are spoken using a specific rhythm and melody and the rhythm and melody give the words more power as you are creating more energy and intention behind them.

Powerful Words

Depending on how practiced and developed your mysticism is, your words and intentions may hold a stronger influence than others. That being said, some words naturally hold more power and influence than others. Interestingly there is one word with in the context of show magic that perhaps holds more power than any other. You have most likely already heard it and have possibly used it a few times before: *abracadabra.*

In the world of fiction, abracadabra has been used by magicians, wizards, and witches alike and this is not unintentional. Abracadabra comes from the ancient Aramaic phrase *avra kehdabra*, meaning *"I will create as I speak."* This relates to the power of the spoken word because when an individual uses words to speak out loud, they are doing so in a way to bring about a specific result.

Because each word has a specific meaning the universe knows how to respond to your intention. How are we to know how the words will influence the world around us? After all, the meaning and definition of words change and evolve so much that many words have departed from their original definition. To truly learn what the meaning of a word is and how to use it to share true meaning and intention, it is suggested that you look into the etymology and history of its use as this can give some great insight into how words should be used and hidden meanings.

Intention, the Spoken Word, and Casting Spells

One last connection that should be explored concerning intention and the spoken word is its relationship with casting spells. Casting a spell, as you will see in the following chapters, almost always includes some sort of enchantment. This enchantment is a collection of words that are spoken out loud which creates sound vibration patterns to influence the energies around you. The enchantments created for certain spells have been specifically designed as such to bring about the most powerful and influential vibration patterns by strategically pushing energy into the world to change certain events.

We must not only be very careful with the enchantments we use and the words we choose for our spells but be as equally careful with the words we choose to speak aloud in out day to day routine. If we are not careful, we may inadvertently speak an enchantment or cast a spell without intention.

Your intention is your goal and the overall aim of exploring mysticism. You will have an overarching and general intention as to why you want to develop your mystic power, in addition to having a specific intention that dictates what you are trying to achieve with each spell and enchantment.

Your intention acts as the fuel to your mystical powers as it helps you discern what you want and helps to aim your magical powers and tools towards the energies you wish to influence. What's more is that since our intention and the words we use to speak our intentions into the world are so powerful, we must be incredibly careful with not only the original meaning behind the words but our intention itself so both forces are aligned. Be sure that your intention is as specific as possible and truly reflects what you wish to manifest into your reality. Otherwise, you may be working to conjure up a reality that you do not want or that can have catastrophic results.

CHAPTER 9

Cleanse and Protect

So far, we have traced the history and lineage of modern-day magic and mysticism and explored the scientific and law-based aspects of mysticism. Now it is time to move to the actual practice of mysticism. Just as there is a very specific starting point when discussing the lineage of magic, there is a starting point when beginning a mystical practice which is to cleanse and protect yourself.

Importance of Cleansing and Protecting

The practice of mysticism comes with responsibility and consequences. Choosing to work with spirits and other realms are recommended for experienced practitioners only. That being said, there are some dangers and precautions that should be taken before any practice or exploration is done. Magic is meant to be benevolent and you should never be practicing magic or any sort of mysticism with the intent to harm others. Moreover, you should never be practicing any sort of mysticism if your intentions – while explicitly benevolent – have hidden harmful repercussions to anyone else. This is where cleansing comes in.

Allow us to explore the cleansing concept with an example. Let us pretend that you spent the day outside gardening and you are covered with soil. However, you have made plans to entertain friends. Rather than simply preparing the food directly after gardening all day, you will want to bathe and cleanse your body of all the dirt. Otherwise, the dirt will contaminate the prepared food. It doesn't matter that the action of preparing food is done with positive intention because the food will still be contaminated. The same philosophy is applied to your magical practice.

Just as you cleanse your body of any dirt or harmful substances, you must cleanse your energy and intentions of any harmful aspects you may have picked up in the world. No matter the good intentions, if there is any negative or malevolent intent present within you, then your magical practice will also be compromised.

On the other hand, you must also protect yourself in your mystical practice. While you can control your intentions and the good deeds and improvements you wish to make, you cannot control the intentions of others. For this reason, you must also learn to protect yourself. Developing your mystical powers requires you to become vulnerable as you turn inward to develop your inner strength as you are engaging with emotions and energies that can be delicate or very susceptible to the energies of others.

Our world is made up of balanced forces and as you reach out into the natural world to develop your mysticism and power, you are likely to face some of those naturally harming and malevolent forces. Depending on the situation, some of these malevolent forces may reach out to you even if you had no intention of reaching out to them, through a book, friend or attractive spell. For this reason, you need to protect your energies from those who are intentionally or unintentionally trying to harm or influence you.

These are the dangers associated with practicing magic and mysticism. You may accidentally work to harm other people or you may be opening yourself up to be harmed by others. For this reason, you must first cleanse and protect yourself before beginning any magical journey and before casting any spell. The rest of this chapter will focus on some suggestions you can use to cleanse and protect yourself appropriately.

Intention Clean-up

As we discussed in the previous chapters, your intention is what you wish to accomplish through your magical spells and enchantments and why you wish to accomplish such a goal. No matter how pure or innocent we think our actions are, we must always evaluate them for hidden biases and negative intentions as it is these hidden intentions that can bring about those negative consequences and harmful results to either ourselves or other people.

To clean our intentions we must first evaluate them as honestly as possible. We should refine them to use wording that is as direct as possible. We must ask ourselves why we want to perform a certain magical enchantment and we should allow for an energy check by a third party to see if there are any subtle or indirect negative energies that we are inadvertently projecting.

Personal Cleanse

If you are familiar with meditation, then the concept of a personal cleanse will not be foreign. What you want to achieve in a personal cleanse is to rid your body of any physical tension held in different joints and muscle groupings in addition to cleansing your mind and your psyche of any hurt feelings or ill-will towards others, let it go. Again, think of cleansing as a washing away of anything that is harming you. This practice is most beneficial when performed in any water source as water is cleansing and purifying.

Performing a Personal Cleanse

To perform a personal cleanse try to imagine someone who is meditating. They are sitting quietly and alone. They are free from any sort of distraction or noise that can interrupt or infiltrate their mind. That being said, a personal cleanse is not the same as meditating, and therefore to perform such a cleanse properly, you should follow these steps:

1. Find a space in your home that provides you with either neutral or positive energy. You want to surround yourself with a natural environment that is free from negative energy.

2. Find a comfortable seat in this space and sit quietly.

3. Search your body for any sort of physical tension; physical tension usually feels like knots or tightness in your body.

4. Take some deep and even breaths and imagine the knots and tightness that you feel in your body unraveling. Once your

body is at peace and rest, is time to turn to your mental and emotional bodies.

5. Search your mental body and emotional self. Evaluate what has happened to you over the past few days and pinpoint any situation that has made you upset or angry – now disengage and view situation objectively.

6. Take a piece of paper and write down all of these situations. They do not have to be incredibly detailed, but you will want to include as much detail as is needed for you to know exactly what the situation is and why it brought about negative emotions.

7. Once you have completed writing out your emotional negativities, fold the paper 4 times and burn it in a fire- safe location.

The idea here is that the burning of your negative thoughts will release them from your body and allow you to be prepared to practice your magic safely.

Protecting Your Home

Protecting your home is the next part of ensuring safe magical practice. It is important to note that although we say 'protect your home,' we mean that you must protect the area and building where you perform your spells and enchantments.

The area where you perform your mysticism acts as a sort of beacon for other magical and mystical entities. Protecting your home allows for blocking of negative or ill intent energies or enities.

To protect your home, you must perform a protection enchantment. Just as a physical fence keeps out physical threats, spiritual protection will keep out spiritual threats. The following is one of the simplest and most effective home protection enchantments to use and employ. Keep in mind that this doesn't necessarily have to be around your home, it just has to be around the building where you practice your mysticism.

1.   Exit your home. You will need to be outside of your home to protect it.

2.   Crouch to the ground and pick up some earth that is around your home. To protect your home, you have to connect with the elements upon which your home rests. If your home is surrounded by water or some other natural element, feel free to take hold of that natural element.

3.   Develop and set an intention for gratitude and appreciation for the Earth underneath your home. It has been working to keep your home spiritually safe. From this gratitude and statement of thanks, develop a type of mantra. Mantras can include a short statement asking for safety and protection, or one that includes your reason why you are asking for protection and what you will be giving back in exchange for the protection.

4. Stand in front of your home. Be sure to visualize the boundary covering the width and length of your home as well to ensure all areas of the building are protected.

By showing your appreciation to the natural world upon which your home rests, you will be placed in alignment with the natural spirits. To draw on the information provided in the previous chapter, this home protection enchantment works alongside the law of compensation, the law of divine oneness, and the law of cause and effect as the natural world will compensate you for showing your appreciation by protecting you and your positive actions will come back as positive rewards.

Protecting Your Energy

In the same way, you want to protect your physical home, you will also want to protect your energies. Your energies are what protect your psyche from being influenced by negative spirits and entities. There are a few different ways to protect your energies but perhaps the most effective is using a talisman.

Talisman

A talisman is an object or thing that you hold with you to bring about a specific incantation or intention. Using talismans to protect your energy is quite simple. First, you will want to take hold of a piece of tree bark as trees are deemed protectors of the forest because they stand strong with their roots deep in the ground which will help to encourage protection.

Once you have taken hold of your talisman, carry it with you at all times especially when you perform any sort of spell or enchantment. To increase the power of the talisman, charge it with your energy and power, you can grasp it in your hands and rub it gently while repeating a protective mantra of your choice.

Be sure that you are visualizing and accepting the protective energy that the talisman is emitting. It will not do well for you to simply hold on to your protective object absent-mindedly and forget about its presence.

Additional Methods That Can Help

There are some other methods that you can use to ensure that your cleansing ritual worked. These additional methods require other objects or actions to take place that are different from enchantments and spells:

Cleansing With Salt

Salt is a natural preservative and can help clean out wounds and sterilize objects. For this reason, it is often used to cleanse energies and different environments.

There are a few different methods you can use when cleansing with salt. First, you can dissolve the salt into some warm water and spray the room with saltwater. Second, you can place sea salt at the entrance and perimeter of your home and property. You could also purchase Himalayan salt lamps for additional cleansing.

Clean Your Home

Another way that you can cleanse is to clean your home. Clutter in your home and surrounding environment leads to clutter in the mind. Every time you move around an object or your eyes fall on the image of clutter, you are cluttering up your mind and your psyche. Just as the physical objects take up space in your home, these object also takes up space in your mind which can compromise and hinder your mystical practices.

Therefore, take part in a monthly house or space cleaning. Get rid of anything that you do not need anymore, and reorganize the items that you want to keep. A monthly clean may seem like a lot but it does not take long for unneeded items to accumulate within your space.

Use Herbs, Plants, and Incense

Perhaps one of the most popular ways of ensuring that your home and your energies are cleansed and protected consistently is to use herbs, plants, and incense. If you can harvest what nature has given to us, it will almost always work in your favor to bring about an improvement in your life.

Placing plants and herbs can help make sure there is always some sort of protection and cleansing happening within the space. Examples of these plants and herbs would be lavender, aloe, cedar, and rosemary. These plants and herbs naturally remove toxins from the air and help to bring in positive energy. Depending on the specific type of protection and what you struggle with most when it comes to cleansing your energy, you should choose your herbs and plants appropriately.

What can also help is burning incense of the same plants and herbs. Incense, like frankincense or lavender, can help soothe any tension that is found within the environment and your body. A list of the most popular and effective herbs for the environment, energy cleansing, and protection can be found at the end of the book.

It is important to protect and cleanse both yourself and your environment before you begin practicing any spell or enchantment. What we have yet to touch on is when such cleansing and protection is needed.

Generally speaking, protection and cleansing spells are not permanent. If you were to never go through another negative experience again, you theoretically wouldn't have to cleanse or protect yourself again. Physical illness, stress and anxiety, heartbreak and loss, and even disagreements with other individuals are unavoidable and inevitable parts of being human. You should look to cleanse and protect both yourself and your environment after any situation or event that has brought on any negative emotions. Examples of these unavoidable situations would be the following:[1]

Illness. Your body and mind are connected deeply and any illness that strikes the body has an effect on the mind and the psyche first. Even if you are just sick with a cold, you will want to re-cleanse your mind

---

[1] https://www.mind-bodygreen.com/0-4398/Easy-Way-to-Cleanse-Your-Home-of-Negative-Energy.html.

as well. Loss. This could be a breakup or the death of a loved one. The heartache and gut-wrenching feelings that you experience during this time will negatively influence your intentions whether you wish them to or not. Anger, disappointment, or stress. No matter how small of a negative experience these feelings may be, it has the power to affect your intention and spiritual practice. Therefore, just to be safe, it is wise to cleanse and protect yourself and the environment. Depression. As creatures of habit, we tend to find comfort in repetition. Sometimes these repetitions can leave us feeling stuck and sluggish. Therefore, anytime you feel like you do not have the same energy or positivity that you should when practicing your mysticism, take the time to perform a protection and cleansing enchantment.

It should also be noted that although you are performing these protections intending to ensure the safety of your mystic practice, performing these rituals during stressful times can also help you move forward and heal from them. Performing a cleansing ritual after you've been in a disagreement with someone could help pull you out of your anger.

Thus, the aspect of protection and cleansing for your mystic practice is perhaps just as important, if not more so, than the rituals and spells you will be casting themselves.

CHAPTER 10

Spell casting

We have moved through the history of paganism and the different variations of pagan religions and belief systems that incorporate a magical and mystical practice. We have also studied the natural laws that allow for the possibility of mysticism to be present within our reality, and we have even moved through certain precautions to take before beginning your practice. It is now time to discuss the practice of mysticism and witchcraft. After all, magic is the ability to bring about change and influence the world at your own will and we cannot explore magic and mysticism without discussing how you can do so.

The practices of mysticism and magic are called spell casting, lorecraft and witchcraft. These practices are referred to as such because how many individuals bring about the change and magically affect their world. To cast a spell is to harness or focused your energy and intention of bringing about a specific outcome while lore craft is predominantly working within the dimension of the Middle World which is governed by universal law. Witchcraft can take many forms but it mainly includes invoking spirits and entities from other dimensions for personal gain. Spell casting can include the use of objects and trinkets to attach or lock in energy. It can also include – and usually does include – the chanting and repeating of a certain phrase or mantra to bring about your change and influence. In other words, spell casting at the basic level is the process of bringing to life and manifesting your intentions.

While we are close to exploring how to practice your spell casting, there are still some precautions to mention first. You will want to start small and slowly if using the spells from others. Even though exploring magic shares its similarities with developing or acquiring any new skill, it is not a skill that you can simply turn off, depending on the agreements you have made and with whom. When you explore mysticism, you are opening yourself up to many forms of information, energy and spirits from many worlds. As a result, once you begin this journey, you will be consistently aware of other worlds. This is not to say that you will always be performing spells and rituals or will be unable to continue your day-to-day life. Rather, it means by agreeing to certain religions, once you connect and open the door you have a responsibility and awareness which can not be undone. Therefore, before you choose to embark further on this journey, be prepared for what it entails. The fundamentals of the book were compiled to serve you and provide the most important information, should you wish to step further or decide to retract completely. Moreover, it is better to begin small and slowly to not overwhelm yourself. There is no rush or need to enter into certain worlds of magic. Take your time and only move forward when you are comfortable and confident to do so as it is harder to remove yourself from the mystical world the deeper you are in it.

Another precaution that must be made before beginning – especially if you are new to the mystic practice – is to try and stay within the limits of your own energies and powers. As you move through with foreign spells and begin to explore your own power, you will be faced with the temptation to invoke and call on the energies of others, in addition to being tempted to purchase spell casting objects and tools. While calling on the energies of others and using objects such as cauldrons or wands can make the development of your power seem more elaborate but these tools are agreements with other religions, they also increase the risk of problems and false improvement. For example, if you call on other energies before fully developing your own inner strength, you may accidentally call on a malevolent spirit and be unable to stop or cleanse yourself of any damage they may inflict. If you rely on objects to perform your spells rather than your own mysticism, you may develop a false sense of confidence and believe you are capable of moving to more intermediate or advanced spells when you are not ready for them. Therefore, be wary and resist the urge to rely on these objects and resist the urge to call on other energies, spirits, and entities as this is completely unnecessary, as you will discover. That being said, if you want to explore further, do so under the supervision of a more experienced mystic.

Before you begin your exploration, please remember to be patient. It takes time to develop your energy and inner power. Over time, you will learn to perfect your power and to do so, you will need to learn patience. Developing your power on your own and working within the limits of your own energies will not only allow you to develop a stronger and more effective practice but also will allow you to be in stronger control of your abilities.

With these precautions in mind, we can now explore how to perform and cast spells.[1] Generally, there are five components needed to properly cast a spell.

Components of Spell Casting

Elements

The first component needed is the elements of the specific spell, which are the elements, objects, and things that are used to perform the specific spell or enchantment.

There is quite a bit of contention surrounding the question of whether or not you should use additional objects to perform your spell. We highly encourage new mystics to stay away such objects in their spell casting practice as it is difficult to harness the power that those objects bring.

That being said, if a new mystic feels comfortable, they should look into using certain herbs and plants to help develop their powers. However, you simply cannot grab whichever herb or plant you wish and cast your spell. Research and gratitude play a large role in herbal magic, and you are encouraged to first learn all you can before embarking on a spell that you have not created. If you take from nature, you must return an offering in its place as the universe is about balance, and reciprocal exchange of energy is required to create harmony. It is important to remember to use only objects that exist

---

[1] Arin Murphy-Hiscock, Spellcrafting: Strengthen the Power of Your Craft by Creating and Casting Your Own Unique Spells (Avon: Adams Media, 2020).

within our world as this will give you a higher chance of being able to control their power.

Our modern world has severed the previously revered connection with nature which has led to a disrespect between individuals and the powers that nature can bring. The energy attached to each living thing has a unique purpose, just like humans have also a gift within us to share. You must always clearly communicate with the plant you wish to use and state your intent as this will allow you to rebuild the respect between mysticism and nature, allowing your powers to develop.

Written Words

The second component of spell casting is the words used to conjure and cast the spell. As mentioned before, the words we use are powerful and must be chosen carefully.

Once we have the intent to change something specific in our lives mystics must write it down. It is this act of writing that solidifies the words as having the potential to be a spell. Once we write it down, that paper and phrase become sacred as those words not only now hold their power as sound vibrations but also hold the potential to be used specifically for change. Once we write down our intention, we must revisit and change it many times before we use it as a spell. Returning and revisiting our words allows us the opportunity to alter the phrasing and word choice to be as specific as possible. After all, the more specific you are with your word choice the less likely we are to yield unintended and unforeseen consequences. If we first write down our intention, it may be marked with unknown negative or compromised energies, and returning to our written phrase gives us the intention to reevaluate our intention as well. Just like having time away from an argument can allow us the opportunity to calm down and view the situation with new eyes, the same results can come about when we write our spells. Never perform magic in haste!

It is also important to do this editing and revision process when the words are written down rather than editing them when we speak them aloud because these potential spells and enchantments have slightly less power and are slightly less dangerous. Words are at their most powerful when they are spoken as it is only then that their sound vibrations are created. Therefore writing down the spell as you edit allows you some time to reflect when the words are safer to change. You may also want to write them using neutral or positive colors to help encourage benevolent and positive energies to be drawn to you. Only once you have edited your written intention and have appropriately charged your body and mind with energy should the words be spoken aloud.

At this point, you may be wondering why you can't use someone else's spells. After all, you can find spells in a spellbook. Why not let someone else do all the hard work?

The answer to this question resides in the question itself: someone else wrote them and the spell in question is full of their intention, not yours. While these spells are published, there is no way of knowing for certain that the original spellcaster's bias and negative energy have been removed from the words. There is much more pride and strength that comes from writing and developing your spells as doing so will help you to become a powerful mystic.

As mentioned during the discussion about the law of agreement, casting a spell is a way of agreeing with the spiritual and natural world. If you use the words chosen by someone else, you are not allowing yourself to fully understand the terms of the agreement. After all, you wouldn't let someone else sign a legal document for you so why would you let someone else choose your spell words? Therefore, when it comes to the word component of spells, you should always formulate your own spells to use, as each will be unique to your situation and desired outcome. You certainly can use other spells for inspiration but when it comes to the actual casting of spells, you should always create your own and go through the editing process. It is the only way to ensure that your intention is pure.

Energy Boosts

Energy boosts are another exciting aspect of casting spells. The energy that you hold within yourself and project out into the world and the energy that you are trying to influence comes into play when we cast spells.

The universal law of oneness states that we are all connected through our energetic life-force. When your energy shifts and evolves, it brings about a shift in the energy of somebody else. In the same way, the shift in your own energy was most likely caused by a shift in somebody else's energy. This energy check-in is often called an energy boost. This name was developed by mystics who focused on producing high, strong, and positive frequencies with their spell casting. When it comes to casting spells, you must perform an energy-boosting ceremony.

The reason for such a ceremony is to utilize the supply of oxygen to energize the positive and negative charges within our bodies. Going through a ceremony that focuses on bringing oxygen into our bodies can boost our energy to help encourage powerful and successful spells. A typical energy-boosting ceremony is as follows:

Begin by standing up straight. You will want your arms and your legs relaxed with your elbows and knees slightly bent. Be sure that you are not slouching as there cannot be any explicit or obvious tension held within your body. Inhale and pay attention to how your body feels as the oxygen fills your lungs. Allow your chest to rise and your abdomen to expand. This is a negative charge. On your exhale, focus on how your body feels as the air leaves your body. Allow your body and chest to contract inward and for your abdomen to come back to rest. This is considered your positive charge. With each inhale, focus on expanding your chest a little bit more as you breathe in. While on your exhale, focus on pushing the air out as your chest comes to rest. With each breath in and every breath out, move your focus from what your body is doing and try to visualize the energy and oxygen itself. Visualize the airflow moving along and down your spine. Once you have mastered picturing your oxygen, you can incorporate the movements of your body along with your breath. For instance, on your inhale, raise your arms above your head and pull them upwards. Stretch your back slightly to allow for the air to flow through your body. On your next exhale, lower your arms once more and feel the air escaping. From this point, you can begin to play with the movements of your body and the feeling of oxygen entering and escaping your body. On your inhale, only raise your right arm above your hand, stretching and expanding only the one side. On the exhale, lower your right arm back to your side. On your next inhale do the same motion again, but this time with your left arm.

Feel free to let your eyes do whatever they naturally wish to. If you feel drawn to closing your eyes during your energy boosting ceremony then do so; if you wish to focus on a distant object or even follow your arm movements with your eyes then you should do so. Once you feel comfortable with the breath work and the movements, it is now time to employ a pause in the breath. Hold your breath for a moment or two after you inhale and before you exhale. This holding of your breath will ensure that the power and energy that is supplied by the oxygen stays within your body and is absorbed. This breathwork should be continued until you can feel your energy levels becoming stronger.

This exercise, like any other, requires time and discipline to grow and perfect. Be patient and soon you will feel this ceremony boosting your energy.

Visualization

The next component of casting spells is visualization. Collecting items and elements that represent and hold certain magical qualities, having a perfect intention, and ensuring that you have high and strong energies are important, but what really drives the success of your spell is your visualization.

Visualization is the act of imagining what you want and what you intend to happen. During your enchantment and repetition of your intention, you should be picturing a few different images and projecting them out into the world. The first is that you should imagine your spell being successful and imagine the feeling of it working. Another visualization technique is imagining you pushing your energies into the world and affecting those worldly energies.

The theory behind the spell casting component of visualization is based on the law of belief. You do not have to only believe what you see. You can believe that your spell will be successful and visualize it as such. This visualization will help to give your spell and intention strength and this increases the chances of the spell being successful.

Closing Down

The last component of casting a spell is to end it. When you begin your spell you open yourself up to creation and the energies around you. If you end your spell by simply stopping the repetition of your intention and enchantment and walking away, you are risking compromising your spell. For this reason, you have to close out your practice. Think about casting a spell as driving a car. To drive your car, you have to turn the car on by turning on the engine. Once you make sure that your settings are correct, you then go through the process of driving. Once you have reached your destination, you not only stop the car but also turn it off before you exit. Closing down a spell has similar steps.

When you begin your spell you are turning on your energies as to affect he world around you. When you are done casting your spell, you have to close out your energies to ensure that no unintended consequences come from it. You also must have a closing intention that states that you have finished your spell. You must also –

depending on what elements you are using for your spell casting – you can burn a different herb or at the very least stop burning your herb to show the energies that your spell casting is done. If you don't close out your practice, then you may be unintentionally casting out energies with the small actions you do after your spell. Remember, the spell has to be as clear and specific as possible.

Furthermore, you have to protect your energies after you have completed your spell. Spell casting is both mentally and physically draining and you must go through the cleansing process again

once your spell is done to continue to protect yourself. This means you should cleanse objects, areas, or places that once had a different owner but now belong to you. You should also get as much rest as you can before and after spell casting to replenish your energy levels.

CHAPTER 11

Discipline

There are three aspects that are needed to have a successful mystic practice and to encourage a strong development of your inner power. The first is knowledge.

The second aspect is the development and practice of your inner power through spells and cleansing.

The third aspect is learning to maintain this power through discipline and the use of a strong moral compass. Being able to manipulate and influence the events in our world mystically is a skill that must be practiced. Very few individuals are able to have such power without actually working to develop it. As a result, you must practice your mystic powers to maintain your skill level. Just as professional athletes need consistent practice and training to ensure that their bodies and skillset stay at the desired ability level, you must also take part in a consistent routine to strengthen your power. This is where the aspect of discipline comes in, which is the idea of you abiding by and following a scheduled practice.

As you may have noticed with maintaining any sort of consistency in your life, developing a strong sense of discipline and consistency is a difficult task to obtain because many factors play into how disciplined you can be. The reason that professional athletes may have an easier time being disciplined is that they devote their entire lives to being perfect at their one skill.

Unless you are looking to become a professional mystic, it is unreasonable to ask that you devote your entire life to your mystical practice and the development of your inner power. That being said, there are some changes to your day-to-day routine and to your life in general that can help you stay consistent with your practice.

Factors Of Discipline

Mind and Body Connection[1]

There is a connection between the mind and the body that is needed to develop your mystical powers. Since mysticism is seen as a supernatural power, many individuals forget about the importance of their physical bodies. Yet, when your physical body is healthy and working seamlessly with your mind, you are more likely to be able to develop a strong mysticism. For this reason, it is suggested that new and established mystics examine their diet. Look for any sort of artificial or chemically based foods and remove them from your diet. Consistently eating genetically modified foods, foods with high sugar,

---

[1] Evelyn Medawar et al., "The Effects of Plant-Based Diets on the Body and the Brain: A Systematic Review," Nature News (Nature Publishing Group, September 12, 2019), https://www.nature.com/articles/s41398-019-0552-0.

and foods that are unhealthy for you can drain your energy stores and produce a negative charge on the body. As a result, an ill body can lead to you experiencing fogginess, poor concentration, and fatigue among many other negative symptoms.

You must ensure the connection between your mind and your body is working seamlessly. While the majority of mysticism is coming from your mind and your psyche, we need to remember that power is also cultivated in the body. Stronger power needs a strong and healthy body and, for this reason, many new and established mystics tend to follow a conscious and healthy eating plan. If you want to go one step further to boost your energy, grow your own food.

Distractions[2]

Another reason why individuals find it difficult to maintain a consistent mystical practice is due to everyday distractions. It is nearly impossible to remove ourselves completely from distractions. Perhaps one of the largest distractions is the sheer amount of technology that surrounds us on any given day. Technology is always within reach and it is very difficult to stop using technology because of how immersed our culture is with it. While there is nothing inherently wrong with technology, it can have a negative effect as it removes consciousness and intention from many actions in our lives.

For this reason, to establish a consistent discipline and practice for your mysticism, it is highly suggested that you reduce or remove

---

[2] Manfred F. R. Kets de Vries, "If You're Feeling Drained, Here's Why," INSEAD Knowledge, November 4, 2019, https://knowledge.insead.e-du/blog/insead-blog/if-youre-feeling-drained-heres-why-12631.

many – if not all – of these technologies from your life. This detox can include removing the television from your bedroom or place of rest, allowing your house to be lit up through natural light rather than ceiling lights or lamps, ditching social media apps from your cellular phone, and reducing any machine applications that are not essential.

Unless you are planning on becoming a career mystic, a complete detox of this nature may seem more inconvenient than beneficial. For this reason, it is recommended to schedule a weekly or monthly detox.

A scheduled detox is when you choose a finite and designated time every week or month to remove any technology from your sight. It could be as simple as removing social media from your phone and utilizing this normally unproductive time by indulging in nature, reconnecting with wild magic during summer evenings, reading books to learn more about the elements, or just decluttering your home. In doing so, you will develop coping mechanisms and strategies to allow you not to be distracted by these external stimuli on a regular basis. After consistent practice, you will notice the return of your concentration and ability to focus clearly!

Motivation

One last factor is motivation. In order to be committed to a consistent practice to develop your own inner power, you have to be motivated to do so. Motivation can be hard to come by and can be a difficult characteristic to maintain, especially in the face of difficulty and challenges.

Practicing mysticism is perhaps one of the most difficult skills to develop because while you are making yourself stronger, you are also making yourself vulnerable to other entities. As you try to influence and affect the events of the world, it may be a while before you see results. However, the faster you detox and start concentrating on personal growth, the more rapid the results will show themselves. The difficulty of developing your powers can lead to a decrease in motivation. Therefore, it is encouraged to explore and develop a system to spark and maintain your motivation when needed.

To be clear, the system that you use to maintain your motivation is meant to be personal. That being said, there are some motivational systems that people find successful. One of these systems is to join a community where your developing skill is nurtured by people. To keep with the example of the professional athlete, athletes find camaraderie with their teammates. It is much easier to train your mind and body towards your sport when your teammates are doing the same thing. The same mindset applies to mysticism.

Another way of maintaining your motivation is to evaluate what motivation means to you and remind yourself of those answers frequently. Just as repetition can help you to perfect your practice, repetition of your intentions and motivation can help you stay in line with what you want to get out of your power. See Appendix 2 at the back of this book for how you can employ this personal exploration of motivation.

If you want to keep a disciplined and consistent practice, you will want to ensure that your energy and attention stays focused towards your practice. Physical illness, a lack of motivation, and submitting and subjecting yourself to society's distractions are all ways that your energy becomes compromised. Fortunately, there are methods and techniques you can employ to ensure that your energies are protected and that your discipline and conviction stay strong.

How to Stay Disciplined

Be Aware and Focused

One way to help maintain your discipline is to be aware and present in the moment. Along the lines of pushing aside distractions, it is important that you stay in the moment of your mystic practices. When you are casting a spell, you want that to be your only focus.

You also want to be self-aware and present in your consciousness. Not only do you want to push aside any distractions but you also want to ensure that your consciousness is in the proper state to perform any sort of spell. To be self-aware means to reflect on your mood and your psychic state. Ensure that you are not holding on to any sort of tension or negative feelings which can infiltrate your mystic practice and skew your intention.

Be Consistent

Another way of staying disciplined is staying consistent. To be consistent requires repetitive and focused practice. The best way to ensure that you stay consistent is to block out a specific time that can be reserved for mystic exercises. You must honor this time to strengthen and further develop your goals. This will allow you to improve your powers and perfect them as well.

Perfection and improvement require repetition and the easiest way to ensure repetition is to schedule it. Although you will be practicing mysticism, it may be wise for you to take cues from an athlete's schedule. They practice every day multiple times a day and the same sort of schedule can and should be applied to your mystical practice.

Be Challenging

Another aspect to ensure the strength of your discipline is to not get bored as boredom is the enemy of development. If your practice becomes too much of a routine, you are more likely to lose interest in it and then you are more likely to stop practicing. Therefore, be sure to include a sense of newness and difficulty into your practice to ensure that you maintain interest.

Including challenges into your mystic practice has a second benefit as well. Development and strength come from overcoming challenges. Just as the weightlifter slowly increases the amount of weight on his barbell to increase his strength, you should want to slowly increase the amount of difficulty in your mystic practice.

Be Patient

One last important factor to consider when you want to maintain your discipline is to remind yourself to be patient. Developing any sort of skill – but especially developing your inner power towards mysticism – takes time. By remove the importance you hold to a certain outcome will free the energy and allow it to flow into existence.

Losing your patience when results come slowly can lead to an abandoned practice. Therefore, you must remind yourself to be as patient as possible with yourself and your practice. Some mystics' skills and spells may take you longer to learn and master than others while others may master a skill quickly but the results of that spell may be slower to be noticed. For this reason, patience is imperative in order to stay disciplined and consistent.

You have to consider your mystic abilities as a skill that must be practiced and a discipline that must be respected. Otherwise, you will lose your motivation and you may be either compromising your ability or your practice might be abandoned altogether.

Final Words

Our society pushes us towards distraction. We are constantly told that we are merely affected by the world around us and at the mercy of reality. As a result, we are bombarded with products and ideas that are meant to help us gain control of our lives to not be so overwhelmed. We do not need all of the external and commercially produced materials and stimuli to calm our lives.

We only need to look within ourselves and develop our power to affect the change we need in our lives. By slowing down and returning to truly experiencing the nature surrounding us we can learn that we are not at the mercy of the universe. Rather, we are in a constant conversation and reciprocal relationship with the universe. We need to learn how to develop this power we have by looking at pagan belief systems that incorporate magic into their practice. By developing your inner magic, you can help to calm your life and free yourself from the helplessness you may feel. Not only will you learn how to change and influence the world around you to improve your life, but you will also find a new sense of community and belonging as you realize your place in our world.

After reading this book, four aspects of magic should be clear to you. First, we are the magic. We are all beings of this realm that can use universal laws and the power of our intention to manifest desires and alter our reality at will. The second is the importance of awareness. As human beings who hold the potential for magic, we need to understand the ancient forms of magic because they highlight our connection to nature and the magical realm. This awareness of past forms of magic means that we also must understand that all things in nature are alive and we can communicate with every single life-force out there to assist our journey. The third is that with this awareness comes the ability to recognize and acknowledge that while other realms and forces exist, we do not need them to alter our reality because they do not belong in this dimension and in doing so comes with a exchange. Our most powerful magic comes from within ourselves, not other people. This is why so much time and money is spent buying our attention in this dimension. The choice to enter into agreements will always be your free will. To track your attention occasionally, ask yourself, who is benefiting from this activity? We don't need to go through anyone or thing to create a wonderful life. Your wonderful life already exists and is waiting for you to believe you are enough. The fourth and last aspect is that magic, and developing our magical powers, is to know ourselves. To know and understand ourselves is what all magic begins and ends with. Being able to understand ourselves – our truest wants, desires, and limits – will prove to be the main source of the power we possess, the key to your own personal magic.

As you move beyond these pages to begin your exploration of yourself, do not forget that magical practice is just that: a practice.

Learning how to communicate with the universe and nurture your inner powers will take time. Therefore, be sure to be consistent with your practice and cultivate a community or individual and tools if you choose to proceed. In this book – we have highlighted the need for caution, understanding thy self and the laws that govern your existence, all the fundamentals you will need to safely navigate your mystical journey. Although we have worked to demystify magic to make it more approachable, remember that magic is still meant to have an aspect of fantasy and creativity. Be sure to enjoy each step of the journey as it can be both challenging yet rewarding but nevertheless will ultimately change your existence forever.

Appendix #1: Herbs and Plants for Cleansing and Protecting

As promised, here is a list of some of the most popular herbs, plants, and incense that can be used to help cleanse and protect you and your home. Pay close attention to what specific negative situation or evil spirit each herb and plant is meant to cleanse and protect you from. You will want to choose them and employ them accordingly to ensure they are effective.[1]

Juniper

Juniper is an herb and berry that is suggested to be burned. It is used to provide an overall comfort for your home and space. Juniper is a scent that is not offensive and is very subtle and to have it consistently burning in your space can provide for protective and cleansing undertones.

---

[1] Dana Claudat, "10 Ways to Clear Your Home of Negative Energy (That Aren't Burning Sage)," mindbodygreen (mindbodygreen, June 25, 2021), https://www.mindbodygreen.com/0-26082/10-ways-to-clear-your-home-of-negative-energy-that-arent-burning-sage.html.

Cedar

Burning cedar can help purify the air when it has been full of dust and musk so it is great to burn when you are decluttering and cleaning your home. It would be great to use cedar in conjunction with the cleansing and protection method of your monthly clean.

Cedar can also be used when you bring new objects into your space as it can help purify the air around the object to not allow the space to become cluttered.

Yerba Santa

Usually used as an herb that is burned or smudged when the individual has experienced a great loss, yerba santa helps to fill a space with positive energy. When we have experienced a great loss, many individuals feel as though there is a part of their emotional and physical bodies that have been empty. By burning this herb, we can help fill that void and empty space with positive energy to help us move on from such loss and heartbreak.

Lavender

As an essential oil, lavender is known to help reduce a person's anxiety and stress. This same effect can happen when it is burned and inhaled as a scent. Therefore, burning lavender incense or having lavender plants within your space can help to have a consistent air of calmness surrounding you. You may also want to increase the usage of lavender when you are going through a stressful time as this will help you to not allow the negative experience to compromise your magical practice.

Sandalwood

At times during your exploration of mysticism, you may feel like you are losing grasp of reality. This is when you should burn sandalwood. The calming smell of sandalwood can help bring you back down to the ground and help you create that foundation you need to have a better grasp on reality.

Lemon

Generally speaking, lemon is a positive smell. Often associated with happiness due to its bright and citrusy, lemon can help bring about positive energies to push out the negative ones.

Spritzing lemon water or burning lemon peel can help to fill your home and your mind with positive energies and smells to not leave room for any negative energy to enter.

Rosemary

You will want to choose rosemary when you are going through any new experiences or making any large change to your life. Rosemary has a steady and calming scent that comforts many individuals with its familiarity. As a result, it can help to calm the nerves and anxiety associated with bringing newness into your life.

Rosemary is also a scent that overwhelms a room. Therefore, when there is any doubt or worry about bringing new change into your life, rosemary will overwhelm and remove these feelings and leave only positive feelings and energies.

Eucalyptus and Peppermint

Eucalyptus and peppermint are often used in naturopathic and homeopathic healing to help clear the sinuses and improve immune systems. Similar uses and applications can be found in witchcraft and mysticism. Since physical illness can compromise your magical ability, burning eucalyptus and peppermint incense or applying eucalyptus and peppermint essential oils to the body can help to boost your immune system and remove any immune-based reasons as to why your magical powers have been compromised.

It should be noted that the list of possible herbs, plants, and incense that you can use to help cleanse and protect your energies in your home is arguably infinite. With its deep roots in natural medicine, even essential oils can be used to heal your energies. Moreover, many of the herbs and plants overlap in their usage. For example, peppermint can also be used to help clear the room of anxious feelings and worry just as lavender can.

Since there are so many options as to which herb or plant you can use, what is important to remember is that there is a personal aspect to it. You should not feel the need to use a specific scent for a specific purpose if the scent is unappealing or sickening. For example, if you do not like the scent of lavender you can opt for peppermint to clear the room of worry. Moreover, be prepared for a series of trial and error. It may take a while for you to find the perfect scent to protect and cleanse against the specific negative emotion and evil spirit.

Therefore, take your time and explore the different herbs and plants available to you in addition to exploring the different methods by which you can use the herbs to fill the space. Remember, practicing mysticism and witchcraft is meant to be an exploration and a journey so take your time and enjoy every aspect of it even if it is simply selecting your protective and cleansing materials.

Appendix #2: Questions to Help Bring About Self-Awareness and Motivation

As discussed in Chapter 11, self-awareness is a key aspect to perfecting your spell casting and developing a sort of discipline surrounding it. Self-awareness will allow you to be present in your practice and not go through the motions. Having a disconnect from yourself – when your mysticism and mystic power are concerned – will lead to a compromised practice.

The following are some questions that you can ask yourself and use to guide your consciousness and awareness back to the moment and encourage the inward turn needed for a successful magical practice.

What does motivation mean to me?

This question is important as it can help you discern what can help motivate you and what tends to be a discouraging factor in your discipline. Figuring out what motivation means to you can lead you to realize that your definition of motivation and consistency differs from others. As a result, you may need different types of motivation to ensure consistent and disciplined practice.

How can I motivate myself and be motivated in general?

Figuring out what motivates you specifically can help keep your goal in line. Naming what motivates you can ensure that you keep those elements of your life around you at all times to maintain your discipline and consistent advancement toward your goal.

Is there something in my life keeping me from feeling motivated?

It is suggested that you examine your life by evaluating your life through an honest lens of whether or not you are happy and motivated. Ask yourself if there are any areas in your life where you feel stuck or you feel as though you lack direction and drive. Analyzing those areas and naming why you do not feel motivated or driven can help you rediscover your intention and inspiration to continue with your magical practice.

Is there something in my childhood or past that is keeping me from being motivated?

You should also gently examine your past and childhood as aspects of your past can give you hints as to why you may be motivated and driven in certain areas while you are easy to give up on others. What is important about this question is that you do not simply pinpoint any sort of childhood trauma or event that can lead to you being unmotivated but you tackled that event and not have it influence your life so much.

Are there any common situational factors that are present when I don't follow through?

This question may be a difficult one to undertake as it requires you to look at your failures. Choose and select a failure that is similar to your goal at hand and evaluate it for the reason as to why such a goal was a failure and not accomplished. This is not meant to make you relive your failure and make you feel bad about it, rather it is meant to be a learning experience and show you how you can improve.

What aspects of others do I admire in their discipline and motivation?

One way to help you develop motivational tools is to keep consistent practice and discipline and to look to those individuals you admire. Ask yourself what they do differently in their life that may help them have a more consistent motivation. You can even try to ask those individuals that you look up to their practices and tools and borrow them to employ them in your own life.

In what ways do I sabotage myself?

Evaluating how you sabotage yourself can also help maintain your motivation through difficult times. Once you have found those patterns of motivation and inactivity in your life, you can examine them for hints and specific actions that hurt your motivation. For example, if you wish to lose weight and you find that you have a destructive pattern of snacking too often, a way that you might be sabotaging yourself is by keeping unhealthy snack foods in your home.

How do I tackle challenges and problems?

One last method to how you can beat your patterns of procrastination and lack of drive can be to evaluate and discover how you look at problems. If you look at challenges as instances of difficulty that you cannot overcome or obstacles, then you may be naturally diminishing your motivation. However, if you see problems as challenges that can help improve and better your ability or skill then you can help to increase your motivation and drive towards your goal.

Answering these questions can not only help bring about self-awareness but help you stay motivated in your practice and discipline of mysticism. Of course, it does not work to simply ask yourself these questions once. Rather you may want to purchase a journal, explore these questions in detail within that journal, and refer back to the answers when you find that you are lacking motivation and discipline in your practice.

What may also be helpful is to ask yourself these questions once a year. As you age and become more experienced within your mysticism, your motivations will change.

References

"5 Ways to Get Rid of Evil Spirits." https://www.pathfor-wardpsychics.com. Accessed October 13, 2021. https://www.pathforwardpsychics.com/article/self-care-and-spirituality/5-ways-to-guard-your-home-from-evil-spirits/7374

"Animism." Animism - an overview | ScienceDirect Topics. Accessed October 8, 2021. https://www.sciencedirect.com/topics/social-sciences/animism.

"Australian Aboriginal Ceremony." Aboriginal Incursions. Accessed October 20, 2021. https://aboriginalincursions.com.au/the-dreaming/aboriginal-ceremony-explained.

Bennett, Andrew. "What We Speak Is What We Create: Andrew Bennett at Tedxtowsonu - Youtube." Accessed October 15, 2021. https://www.youtube.com/watch?v=BVK4mWaS3F8.

Blakemore, Erin. "Druids-Facts and Information." History. National Geographic, May 3, 2021. https://www.nationalgeographic.com/history/article/why-know-little-druids.

Carter, Joe. "9 Things You Should Know about Wicca and Modern Witchcraft." The Gospel Coalition, May 22, 2018.

https://www.thegospelcoalition.org/article/9-things-you-should-know-about-wicca-and-modern-witchcraft/.

Claudat, Dana. "10 Ways to Clear Your Home of Negative Energy (That Aren't Burning Sage)." mindbodygreen. mindbodygreen, June 25, 2021. https://www.mindbodygreen.com/0-26082/10-ways-to-clear-your-home-of-negative-energy-that-aren't-burning-sage.html.

"Contract." Legal Information Institute. Legal Information Institute. Accessed October 15, 2021. https://www.law.cornell.edu/wex/contract#:~:text=Definition,consideration%3B%20ca-pacity%3B%20and%20legality.

Coughlin, Sara. "How 4 Witches & Wiccans Define Their Faith for Themselves." Real Witches Talk About Their Wiccan Religion & Beliefs. Accessed October 8, 2021. https://www.refinery29.com/en-ca/real-witches-wiccan-religion-beliefs.

"Deidre Madsen's Award-Winning Author of Happily Inner After." law of mentalism. Accessed October 9, 2021. http://deidremadsen.com/happilyinnerafter/index.php/component/tags/tag/411-law-of-mentalism.

"Druids." Myths Encyclopedia. Accessed October 8, 2021. http://www.mythencyclopedia.com/Dr-Fi/Druids.html.

Estrada, Jessica. "How to Harness the Power of the 12 Laws of the Universe to Improve Your Life." Well+Good, August 27, 2021. https://www.wellandgood.com/laws-of-the-universe/

Faragher, Aliza Kelly. "A Beginner's Guide to Casting Your Own Spells." Allure, March 26, 2018. https://www.allure.com/story/how-to-cast-spells.

Ferraro, Kris. "Easy Ways to Cleanse Your Home of Negative Energy." mindbodygreen. mindbodygreen, December 29, 2020. https://www.mindbodygreen.com/0-4398/Easy-Way-to-Cleanse-Your-Home-of-Negative-Energy.html.

Habits and Customs. Accessed October 20, 2021. http://rimstead-cours.espaceweb.usherbrooke.-ca/ANG4562/site/page%203.htm.

Hall, Emily. "What Is Wicca? History, Beliefs, and Rituals (plus What the Bible Says)." Christianity.com. Christianity.com, April 5, 2019. https://www.christianity.com/wiki/cults-and-other-religions/what-is-wicca-history-beliefs-and-rituals-plus-what-the-bible-says.html.

Halstead, John. "We're Not All Witches: An Introduction to Neo-Paganism." HuffPost. HuffPost, December 7, 2017. https://www.huffpost.com/entry/were-not-all-witches-an-i_b_8228434.

Hart, Avery. "Animism: What Is It and How Can You Use It?" The Traveling Witch, July 13, 2021. https://thetravelingwitch.com/blog/animism-what-is-it-and-how-can-you-use-it.

Hays, Jeffrey. "Animism and Shamanism." Facts and Details. Accessed October 12, 2021. https://factsanddetails.com/world/cat55/sub350/item1918.html

"Here Are the Steps to Casting Spells That Unquestionably Work." Home. Accessed October 17, 2021. https://www.semasan.com/sema/inc/?here_are_the_steps_to_castin g_spell-s_that_unquestionably_work.html.

"History of the Druids: Ancient Druids." Order of Bards, Ovates & Druids, November 25, 2020. https://druidry.org/druid-way/what-druidry/a-longer-history.

History.com Editors. "Wicca." History.com. A&E Television Networks, March 23, 2018. https://www.history.com/topics/religion/wicca.

iTrueHealthy. "Magic Words - How Words Can Be Used as Magic Spells." YouTube. YouTube, July 1, 2017. https://www.youtube.com/watch?v=FzYwuifw1O4.

John Beckett. "Ancestor Work." John Beckett. Patheos Explore the world's faith through different perspectives on religion and spirituality! Patheos has the views of the prevalent religions and spiritualities of the world., April 14, 2021. https://www.patheos.com/blogs/johnbeckett/2021/04/ancestor-work.html.

"The Law of Agreement." Bill Winston Ministries. Accessed October 15, 2021. https://www.billwinston.org/The-Law-of-Agreement/.

Manfred F. R. Kets de Vries. "If You're Feeling Drained, Here's Why." INSEAD Knowledge, November 4, 2019. https://knowledge.insead.edu/blog/insead-blog/if-youre-feeling-drained-heres-why-12631.

Medawar, Evelyn, Sebastian Huhn, Arno Villringer, and A. Veronica Witte. "The Effects of Plant-Based Diets on the Body and the Brain: A Systematic Review." Nature News. Nature Publishing Group, September 12, 2019. https://www.nature.com/articles/s41398-019-0552-0.

Melina, Remy. "What's Witchcraft? 6 Misconceptions about Wiccans." LiveScience. Purch, August 23, 2013. https://www.live-science.com/39119-myths-about-witches-wiccans.html.

"Mortgage (n.)." Etymology. Accessed October 15, 2021. https://www.etymonline.com/word/mortgage.

Murphy-Hiscock, Arin. Spellcrafting: Strengthen the Power of Your Craft by Creating and Casting Your Own Unique Spells. Avon: Adams Media, 2020.

"The Native American." Native American Pipe Ceremony. Accessed October 13, 2021. http://www.native-americans-online.com/native-american-pipe-ceremony.html.

NHS choices. NHS. Accessed October 8, 2021. http://www.waht.nhs.uk/en-GB/NHS-Mobile/Our-Services/?depth=4&srcid=2007.

"Paganism a Brief Overview of the History of Paganism the ..." Accessed October 8, 2021. https://americanhumanist.org/wp-content/uploads/2016/11/paganism.pdf.

Psychic Elements Author - Psychic Elements Staff. "The 12 Spiritual Laws of the Universe." Psychic Elements - Psychics Blog, October 10, 2017. https://psychicelements.com/blog/the-12-spiritual-laws-of-the-universe/.

"Religions - Paganism: Wicca." BBC. BBC, October 2, 2002. https://www.bbc.co.uk/religion/religions/pagan-ism/subdivisions/wicca.shtml.

Sheloya. "Sheloya." Witch University, August 5, 2017. http://witchuniversity.com/2017/start-with-cleansing-and-protection-for-witchcraft-beginners/.

Staff, Christianity.com Editorial. "Who Are Pagans? the History and Beliefs of Paganism." Christianity.com. Christianity.com, September 23, 2019. https://www.christianity.com/wiki/cults-and-other-religions/pagans-history-and-beliefs-of-paganism.html.

Taylor, Brian. "Telepathy (Feeling at a Distance): Animism, Healing, and Science." animist jottings, March 19, 2017. https://animistjottings.wordpress.com/2015/02/19/telepathy-feeling-at-a-distance-animism-healing-and-science/

"What Is Animism?" Ethnos360. Accessed October 8, 2021. https://ethnos360.org/magazine/stories/what-is-animism.

"What Is Paganism?" Pagan Federation International, June 5, 2020. https://www.paganfederation.org/what-is-paganism/.

"The Wheel of the Year in the Druid Tradition – Description of Druidic Holidays." The Druid's Garden, August 12, 2016. https://druidgarden.wordpress.com/2013/04/06/the-wheel-of-the-year-in-the-druid-tradition-description-of-druidic-holidays/.

"When Casting Spells, Must You Provide All of the Components?" Role-playing Games Stack Exchange, November 1, 1965. https://rpg.stackexchange.com/questions/105123/when-casting-spells-must-you-provide-all-of-the-components.

"Who Were the Druids?" Historic UK. Accessed October 8, 2021. https://www.historic-uk.com/HistoryUK/HistoryofWales/Druids/.

"A Wiccan Guide to Magic: What Is Magic?" Wicca Living, November 6, 2017. https://wiccaliving.com/what-is-magic/.

Yardney, Michael. "The Law of Belief." Property Update, October 17, 2017. https://propertyupdate.com.au/the-law-of-belief/ " Druidism." The Mystica, October 1, 2020. https://www.the-mystica.com/druidism/.

Printed in Great Britain
by Amazon

14904686R00078